Present Yourself 2

Viewpoints

Teacher's Manual

Steven Gershon

CAMBRIDGE
UNIVERSITY PRESS

CAMBRIDGE UNIVERSITY PRESS
Cambridge, New York, Melbourne, Madrid, Cape Town, Singapore, São Paulo, Delhi

Cambridge University Press
32 Avenue of the Americas, New York, NY 10013-2473, USA

www.cambridge.org
Information on this title: www.cambridge.org/9780521713313

It is normally necessary for written permission for copying to be obtained *in advance* from a publisher. The language summaries, outline worksheets, peer evaluation form, assessment form, and audio scripts at the back of this book are designed to be copied and distributed in class. The normal requirements are waived here and it is not necessary to write to Cambridge University Press for permission for an individual teacher to make copies for use within his or her own classroom. Only those pages which carry the wording '© Cambridge University Press' may be copied.

First published 2008

Printed in Hong Kong, China, by Golden Cup Printing Company Limited

A catalog record for this publication is available from the British Library

ISBN 978-0-521-71330-6 student's book and audio CD
ISBN 978-0-521-71331-3 teacher's manual

Cambridge University Press has no responsibility for the persistence or accuracy of URLs for external or third-party Internet Web sites referred to in this publication, and does not guarantee that any content on such Web sites is, or will remain, accurate or appropriate.

Cover and book design: Adventure House, NYC
Text composition: Page Designs International

Contents

Teaching notes

Photocopiable resources

Plan of the Student's Book

Getting ready pages 2–7	**Preparing to present**	**Introducing a classmate**
	Doing a survey to get to know classmates	Completing a brainstorming map
	Learning about the steps for a presentation	Learning about the organization of a presentation
		Listening to a classmate introduction

Unit	**Topic** focus	**Language** focus	**Organization** focus
1 **A motto for life** pages 8–19	Discussing people's mottoes Talking about personal values	Explaining the meaning of a motto Relating a motto to a past experience	All units include focusing on brainstorming ideas and creating an outline for a presentation.
2 **Young people today** pages 20–31	Talking about survey topics, questions, and results Surveying classmates	Describing a survey Reporting survey results	
3 **Dream vacation** pages 32–43	Discussing types of vacations Planning the perfect vacation	Talking about vacation destinations Talking about activities and accommodations	
4 **How the world works** pages 44–55	Taking a trivia quiz Talking about process topics	Introducing a process presentation Explaining a process	
5 **In my opinion** pages 56–67	Discussing issues Completing an opinions survey	Relating an issue and expressing an opposing opinion Supporting opinions	
6 **In the news** pages 68–79	Talking about news headlines Words to describe news stories	Introducing news stories Talking about details in news stories	

Presentation tips	My classmate introduction
An introduction to what good presenters do	Preparing and giving a classmate introduction

Presentation focus	Presentation skills focus	Present yourself!
All units include focusing on the introduction, body, and conclusion of a presentation, and listening to a model presentation.	Making and using presentation notes Tip: Making eye contact when speaking	Brainstorming ideas Creating an outline Giving a presentation about a personal motto
	Explaining visual aids Tip: Using visual aids effectively	Brainstorming questions and doing a survey Creating an outline Giving a presentation about the survey results
	Asking lead-in questions Tip: Timing and intonation of lead-in questions	Brainstorming ideas Creating an outline Giving a presentation about a dream vacation
	Inviting audience questions Tip: Answering audience questions	Researching a process Creating an outline Giving a presentation about the process
	Emphasizing an opposing opinion Tip: Using body language to emphasize an opinion	Brainstorming ideas Creating an outline Giving a presentation about an important issue
	Leading a group discussion Tip: Encouraging audience participation	Researching a news story Creating an outline Giving a presentation about the news story

Introduction

Present Yourself is a presentation skills course for adult and young adult learners of English. The book takes a process approach to giving presentations and combines careful language control with communicative activities that are familiar to students. *Present Yourself* offers students an opportunity to develop the life skill of talking about topics to an audience outside the language classroom.

Present Yourself 2, Viewpoints is intended for intermediate students and focuses on giving presentations that express an opinion or point of view. It can be used as a main text in a presentation skills course, in the context of a general conversation course, or as a component in speaking or integrated-skills classes.

About the book

Present Yourself 2, Viewpoints focuses on topics that encourage students to speak about points of view beyond their personal experiences. The book includes six main units and one introductory unit. The introductory unit acquaints students with the process of planning a presentation, and offers an entry point to giving a presentation by having students introduce a classmate. Each of the six main units guides students through the entire presentation process with engaging speaking activities, focused listening activities that provide relevant topic input, and clear functional language support that targets both vocabulary and useful sentence patterns. Moreover, the core of each unit provides a complete model presentation that students use to help them construct their own presentations based on that unit's topic.

The topics of the six main units are loosely graded by level of difficulty, from presenting survey results in Unit 2, to explaining a process in Unit 4, to talking about a news story in Unit 6. However, as we all know, every class is different, so feel free to pick and choose units according to your students' interests, class level, and available time.

Present Yourself follows a carefully designed process approach. It recognizes that an effective presentation is the result of an individualized process involving a number of related phases. In *Present Yourself*, emphasis is placed on guiding students through the presentation process step by step. The basic elements of this process are, to a large degree, responses to essential questions, from *What do I talk about?* and *Who is my audience?* to *What language and vocabulary do I need for this topic?* to *How do I structure my presentation?* to *What's the best way to deliver my presentation?* And finally, *What changes should I make so my presentation is better next time?*

The aim of this process approach is to provide students with a set of transferable tools within a practical framework that will help them to brainstorm, prepare,

organize, deliver, and evaluate their own presentations, whatever the topic and purpose. To this end, each unit of *Present Yourself* focuses on a presentation topic and guides students through the entire presentation process, lesson by lesson, thereby continually reinforcing the steps and making the framework more and more familiar.

Unit organization

Getting ready

Getting ready is an introductory unit that gives students an opportunity to get to know their classmates so that they will feel more comfortable when they give their presentations in class. The activities help students think about the steps in the process of planning a presentation. They listen to a simple model of a classmate introduction presentation and are gently guided through the process of planning their classmate introduction presentations, which they practice and then give in small groups.

How a unit works

Each main unit of *Present Yourself 2, Viewpoints* contains six lessons to guide students through the process of building an effective and engaging presentation. Each of the lessons, with the exception of the first lesson, builds on the previous one to provide students with the necessary skills to create and deliver their own presentations. Students finish by completing the corresponding **Self-evaluation form** at the back of the book.

Topic focus

This lesson helps students to think about the topic and what they already know about it. The activities introduce useful topic-based vocabulary and encourage students to interact with each other through surveys, questionnaires, quizzes, and interviews. When students finish this lesson, they will have generated ideas that they can use later in the unit when they begin to plan their own presentations.

Language focus

This lesson encourages students to notice useful target expressions and sentence patterns they can use to talk about the unit topic. Students also listen to different speakers use the target language in the context of giving a presentation, and perform task-based listening activities. Students consolidate the target language through a semicontrolled speaking activity at the end of the lesson.

Organization focus

This lesson teaches students how to select ideas from a brainstorming map and organize them into a presentation outline that includes an introduction, a body, and a conclusion. Students are asked to notice which ideas from brainstorming notes have been included as main topics in an outline and to complete the outline with additional notes. Finally, students have an opportunity to listen to the complete presentation as they check the completed outline.

Presentation focus

In this lesson students focus on a model presentation written from the outline in the **Organization focus**. Students focus on the introduction, body, and conclusion of the presentation to see what information is included in each section. While looking at a cloze version of the model presentation, students predict the items to complete each section. They then listen to the complete presentation and check their answers.

Presentation skills focus

At this stage of the unit, students are ready to focus on a specific linguistic or physical skill related to the actual delivery of their presentation. In each unit the presentation skill is first presented visually. The activities vary depending on the presentation skill, but in every unit students observe the presentation skill in action, and then they have an opportunity to practice the presentation skill with a partner, or in a group, in a controlled speaking activity.

Present yourself!

In the last lesson of the unit, students plan, organize, and give their own presentations based on the unit topic. First, students brainstorm ideas for their topic and create an outline for their presentation. Then they practice on their own before giving their presentations to the whole class or in a group.

Self-evaluation forms

The **Self-evaluation forms** on pages 80–85 of the Student's Book may be used at the end of each unit, after students have given their presentations. These forms allow students to reflect upon and evaluate their own presentations in terms of preparation, content, and delivery. Students write comments about what they did well and ideas to help themselves improve in the future. As the forms are intended for students' own use, it is not necessary to collect them. However, you may want to do so after students have completed the forms and respond with your own written comments. Have students look back at the **Self-evaluation form** from the previous unit before they begin planning each successive presentation.

Course planning and flexibility

Present Yourself has been designed to be used in a variety of teaching situations. The six main units in each level are arranged roughly in order of gradually increasing challenge, both in terms of language and presentation

skills. However, the presentation topic of each unit is completely independent from other units and can easily stand alone. Therefore, although it might be ideal to cover all the units in order, feel free to cover the units in any order you think will most benefit your class. Moreover, if you have limited time, large classes, or lower-level students who need more time to fully cover a unit, feel free to skip over any units that you don't have time to cover. You may also choose to have students study only the **Presentation skills focus** lesson of units that they don't have time to fully cover in class. This would give students the full range of presentation skills that they can use for the presentation assignments you choose to include.

Lesson planning

Each main unit of *Present Yourself* represents a series of linked lessons, beginning with the **Topic focus** and ending with the **Present yourself!** lesson. For 90-minute classes, if each unit lesson is covered fully in class, it will take five to six classes to bring students to the point where they prepare and give their own presentations based on the unit topic. However, every class is different in terms of the interests and levels of students, as well as the available time for the course. Therefore, *Present Yourself* offers the flexibility to increase or decrease the amount of time spent on each unit. This can be done in a number of ways:

Expanding the time spent on each unit

- Have students submit their presentation outlines or even a full first draft of their presentations for feedback from you or their classmates before giving their presentations. This will effectively add a useful revising or editing phase or lesson to the presentation process.
- When working on the final **Present yourself!** lesson, have students complete all the brainstorming, planning, and preparation for their presentations during lesson time. This will allow you to oversee and offer help during the entire planning phase. You could also spend some time during this lesson reviewing the presentation skills from the **Presentation skills focus** lessons in previous units.
- Once students have completed the planning and preparation for their presentations during the **Present yourself!** lesson, set up a "rehearsal" lesson during which students can practice their presentations in small groups. This will allow students to get informal feedback from their classmates, make changes to the content, and work on their delivery before giving their presentations more formally in front of the whole class.
- If equipment is available, you may choose to record or videotape all or a select number of student presentations. Then, after students have given their presentations, set up a postpresentation evaluation session, with students watching selected presentations while you elicit their perceptions of the main strengths

and weaknesses of the presentations as a whole. Alternatively, this follow-up evaluation session could be done from memory, without video, either as a whole-class activity or in small groups, with each group reporting back to the class at the end of a discussion period.

Limiting the time spent on each unit

- With students at a higher proficiency level, skip one or more of the activities in the **Topic focus** and **Language focus** lessons. This would mean that these two lessons could be combined and covered in one lesson instead of two.
- Have students do the **Organization focus** lesson (completing the brainstorming notes and presentation outline) as homework. Then, the next time the class meets, you can spend a little more time checking students' answers before moving on to the **Presentation focus** lesson.
- While covering the final **Present yourself!** lesson, have students do either some or all of their presentation planning as homework. This means that students will complete the **Presentation skills focus** lesson in class, and then the next time the class meets, students will give their presentations.
- Any or all of the student presentations may be done in small groups of four to six students rather than in front of the whole class one student at a time. For example, with a class of 30 students, there could be 5 groups doing their presentations at the same time. This means that the whole class could complete their presentations within one lesson and still have time for a follow-up feedback session. This format makes detailed grading and feedback for each individual student more difficult. You may choose to do the presentations in one or two of the units in this format, while giving more detailed individual feedback and grades to each student for the remaining presentations that they do in front of the whole class.

General teaching tips

Maximizing English in the classroom

Although *Present Yourself* focuses on developing students' presentation skills, it is also important to see the course goals as improving students' general communicative competence. Many of the activities, particularly in the **Topic focus** and **Language focus** lessons, directly address these communicative aims. However, there are also many other opportunities during a lesson to maximize and extend the students' functional use of English. Aside from using English as much as possible for simple classroom instructions, explanations and procedures, you can encourage students to use English when asking you for language help and when talking to each other while doing activities. A good way to do this is to provide some useful classroom expressions at the beginning of the course and then spend a little time getting students to practice them. Here are some examples:

Getting help:
What does (word) mean?
How do you spell (word)?
How do you pronounce this word?
How do you say (word) in English?
Can you play it / the CD again, please?
Can you turn it / the CD up, please? (I can't hear it.)

Finding a partner for pair work:
A: *Do you have a partner?*
B: *No, not yet.*
A: *OK, let's work together for this activity.*

Forming groups:
A: *We need one / two more in our group.*
B: *OK, can I join your group?*

Comparing answers:
A: *What did you get for (number 1)?*
B: *I got (answer). How about you?*
A: *I got (answer), too.*
   or
   I don't know the answer.

Deciding the timing for activities

Although suggestions are given in the unit teaching notes for how long activities may normally take to complete, every class is different. Therefore the timing of each activity is flexible, depending on the program syllabus, the level and interest of students, and your goals as a teacher. Activities can be shortened if necessary, or extended by utilizing all the optional warm-up and follow-up ideas offered in the unit teaching notes. In general, it is helpful to let students know how much time they will have to complete an activity, and then to let them know when they have one or two minutes left.

Giving students "thinking time"

When new material or a new activity is introduced, students need time to think before they can be expected to respond. This is particularly important for lower-level or less confident students. The unit teaching notes always suggest that you read the activity instructions aloud first. This is to give students time to absorb what they are being asked to do. It is also a good idea to give students enough time to look at the pictures, scan the questions in charts, digest the language in boxes, or read the model language before asking them to carry out the activity or respond orally. By being attentive to students' facial expressions and body language, you will usually know when most of the class has had enough time to absorb the material and is ready to move on with the activity.

Using visuals (pictures) to activate schema

The Student's Book contains many pictures that introduce the topic of each unit. Visuals can go a long way in helping students to activate their schema – that is, to build on their background knowledge about the topic. This is especially important during brainstorming and planning stages, as well as during prelistening activities. It is always helpful to give students a few minutes to take in a picture fully, mentally describe what is in the picture, and then share their ideas with a partner. There are many ideas in this Teacher's Manual's unit teaching notes to help you exploit the pictures in the classroom.

Checking answers in pairs

The unit teaching notes often suggest that students should be encouraged to share their answers with a partner before you elicit answers from the whole class. This will help to create a more interactive and collaborative class atmosphere. It will also allow lower-level students to be on a more equal footing when you elicit answers from the whole class, especially for listening activities. The first few times students do this, you may want to refer them to the relevant functional expressions from the *Maximizing English in the classroom* section on page viii.

Modeling activities and language

To help students understand and respond to activities, the unit teaching notes often ask you to model the activity or target language. The purpose is not to give students sentences to memorize, but rather to show how to do the activity. Modeling an activity with one of the higher-level students in the class is a useful, efficient way to demonstrate how an activity works. Remember that showing is always much more effective than telling. As the English saying goes, "A picture is worth a thousand words."

Forming pairs and groups

Many of the activities in the Student's Book are for pairs or groups. Students should not always work with the same partner or group. Instead, you can manage the speaking activities so that students move around and talk to different classmates. Getting students to talk to many different classmates will not only help to reinforce their English but also make the lessons more interesting. One way to have students change partners is simply to have every other row of students turn around to face the row behind. Or you can have students rotate in different directions. If students are seated around a large table, they can simply rotate positions around the table. You may also have students simply stand up and move around the room to find a new partner who is not normally seated near them. The first few times students do this, you may want to refer them to the relevant functional expressions from the *Maximizing English in the classroom* section on page viii.

If an activity requires pairs or even-numbered groups, but there is an odd number of students in the class, have one student share the role of another student, each taking turns to respond to their partner. Alternatively, you could be the partner of the extra student, though this will make monitoring other students more difficult.

Monitoring and helping

The unit teaching notes frequently suggest that teachers monitor students' activities. This is to make sure students remain on task and to help individual students, pairs, or groups that are having difficulty. It also helps get a sense of when most of the students have finished an activity. To monitor effectively, it's a good idea to move around the classroom, sitting or standing near pairs or groups and checking that they are doing the activity correctly and using appropriate language. If students are working too slowly or having difficulty expressing themselves, you can briefly join in the pair or group activity. Alternatively, you can pause the activity to explain or model the activity again, before moving on to a new pair or group. You may also choose to keep notes, in a notebook or on a seating chart, about the strengths and weaknesses of particular students in case they need extra help. You may also want to jot down notes about particular activities for future reference.

Using note cards

When making a presentation, students often try to memorize their full presentation. This is understandable, especially when speaking in a second language. However, if they forget one small part, or even a few words, of their "script," they can quickly become paralyzed, with their mind completely blank, while silently trying to remember what comes next.

To avoid this frightening situation, students often want to write out the full text of their presentation on a piece of paper, word-for-word, to have in front of them when they are presenting. Once again, this is understandable. However, when students have the complete word-for-word text in front of them, they tend to read out large chunks of the text from the paper – with their eyes cast down, locked onto the paper instead of the audience. Moreover, their voice takes on a monotonous, flat, "reading" intonation that effectively puts the audience to sleep.

It is therefore a good idea, from the beginning of the course, to encourage students to make note cards to follow when they present. You can specify the maximum size of the note cards that students may use and encourage them to include the main points and bulleted details on the cards. You may also want to show the students examples of note cards with key points highlighted in color or underlined. Speaking from notes is a valuable skill, and the more students practice this skill, the more comfortable they will be with it – and the more effective their presentations will be.

Dealing with nerves

Almost everyone gets nervous when speaking in front of a group. This is natural, even for native speakers. Students will most likely be a little anxious at the beginning of the course, especially if they don't know each other very well. It is therefore vital to create a comfortable, nonthreatening, collaborative learning environment, with a lot of encouragement and praise for the students' efforts. You can also help to decrease this initial anxiety by doing plenty of ice-breaking "get-to-know-you" activities in the first few lessons. This will "lighten" the class atmosphere and encourage students to view their classmates as a friendly, supportive audience for their presentations. *Getting ready*, the introductory unit of *Present Yourself*, contains ice-breaking activities to serve this purpose. You are also encouraged to add your own favorites.

When it comes time to give their presentations, most students will no doubt suffer some stage fright. There are a number of ways to help students deal with this:

- Make sure students realize that some nervousness is completely normal when speaking in public. You may want to have students practice their presentations in small groups first, allowing them to build confidence by practicing in an informal environment.
- Deep breathing can also be used to help decrease nervousness. Taking a few deep breaths silently just before beginning to speak is a great way to calm nerves and start with a strong voice. When students are preparing their first presentation, have them practice walking to the front of the room, facing the class, and taking two or three deep breaths before saying their first sentence. A simple reminder to take a few breaths before each presentation should help students deal with nerves.
- Have students stand up straight with a confident posture and practice making eye contact with their classmates. A confident posture translates into a confident speaker.
- Encourage students to speak slowly and calmly. When nervous, people tend to speak quickly, as if they want to finish as soon as possible. Having students practice speaking calmly also helps reduce nervousness.
- Depending on your students' personalities, you may also want to encourage them to add a little humor to their presentation. Getting some smiles or a laugh from the audience toward the beginning of a presentation does a lot to calm nerves and build confidence. Humor is a great ice-breaker!
- Most important, let students know at the beginning of the course that good, solid preparation and practice is the very best way to decrease their nervousness about presenting. The more prepared they are, the more confident they will feel presenting to an audience.

How to use this Teacher's Manual

This Teacher's Manual contains the following materials:

- Step-by-step teaching notes for each unit in the *Present Yourself 2, Viewpoints* Student's Book
- Language summaries
- Outline worksheets
- Peer evaluation form
- Assessment form
- Student's Book audio scripts for all recorded listening activities

Unit teaching notes

Each Teacher's Manual unit begins with a brief overview describing the aims of each lesson of the corresponding Student's Book unit. In addition to detailed teaching instructions for each activity, the unit teaching notes contain lists of useful vocabulary and language that students will encounter in the activities, as well as helpful teaching suggestions and tips for explaining specific grammar points and cultural references.

Language summaries

There is one photocopiable **Language summary** on pages 52–57 for each corresponding unit in the Student's Book. These summaries list the important words, phrases, and expressions from each lesson, as well as helpful language students will need to use in their presentations. You may want to hand out a copy of the unit's **Language summary** to each student before you begin the **Present yourself!** lesson in each unit. Encourage students to review the vocabulary and to refer to the helpful language as they plan their presentations.

Outline worksheets

The photocopiable **Outline worksheets** on pages 58–63 of this Teacher's Manual are designed to be used in class while students are giving their presentations. Students take notes on their classmates' presentations, which allows them to actively engage in the presentations as they listen. The worksheets help students focus on the content of the presentations, and the process of taking notes helps students listen intently for details and retain the information they hear. Each worksheet follows the same structure as the planning outline in the **Present yourself!** lesson of the corresponding Student's Book unit, so students will be familiar with the organization and topics.

Using the Outline worksheets

- Before students give their presentations, decide how many **Outline worksheets** each student will complete. You may want to limit the number to two or three presentations.
- Have students draw names to decide which classmates' presentations they will take notes on. Alternatively, allow students to choose the presentations on their own.
- Hand out the appropriate number of copies of the worksheet to each student in the class.
- Have students read the topics on the worksheet and explain that they should complete the outline with details from the presentation as they listen. After the presentation, they should complete the last section of the worksheet: *Something else I'd like to know about the topic.*
- Collect the worksheets after all students have given their presentations. You may want to hand them back with written comments and count them as an in-class assignment or a participation grade.

Peer evaluation form

The photocopiable **Peer evaluation form** on page 64 is designed to be used in class after students' presentations to give students a chance to learn from the process of assessing their peers' work. It also provides students with an opportunity to receive helpful feedback from their classmates.

Using the Peer evaluation form

- Before students give their presentations, assign each student two classmates' presentations to evaluate. Make sure each student in the class will receive evaluations from two other classmates.
- Hand out two copies of the form to each student.
- Have students read the criteria on the form, and explain that they should listen carefully to their assigned classmate's presentation and then complete the form.
- Have students give their completed forms to the appropriate classmates after all the presentations are finished.
- Encourage students to read their evaluations and to keep them for future reference.

Assessment form

The photocopiable **Assessment form** on page 65 is designed to help you assess students' presentations as you watch them in class. The form is divided into the three main areas students focus on as they progress through each Student's Book unit: preparation, content, and delivery. You may use the form either as a formal assessment tool or to provide students with informal written feedback.

Using the Assessment form

- Before students give their presentations, make one copy of the form to assess each student in the class.
- Familiarize yourself with the criteria on the form.
- As you watch students' presentations, mark the score for each section accordingly (1 = lowest score; 5 = highest score)

- Calculate and write the score out of a possible 40 points in the space provided.
- Use the section at the bottom of the form at the end of each presentation to summarize each student's strengths and make suggestions for future improvements.
- If you choose to assign a formal grade to the presentation, divide each student's score by 40 points to calculate a percentage. For example, if a student's score is 32, calculate $32 \div 40 = 80\%$.

Student's Book audio scripts

The audio scripts on pages 66–72 of this Teacher's Manual correspond to the listening activities in the **Language focus**, **Organization focus**, **Presentation focus**, and **Presentation skills focus** lessons in the Student's Book. Before doing a listening activity with students, you may want to preview the audio scripts so that you can readily answer any questions students may have about the language or content presented. These pages are photocopiable, and you may hand them out to students for in-class or at-home study if you wish.

From the author

I do hope you enjoy teaching *Present Yourself* and that your students find the topics and activities in this course both interesting and useful. I am confident that by the end of the course, your students will be making effective, engaging presentations they can be proud of.

I would be happy to receive any comments about *Present Yourself* that you or your students would like to share.

Best regards,
Steven Gershon

Getting ready

Overview

In this introductory unit, students interview classmates to find out about one another's backgrounds, interests, and experiences. They also identify the steps in planning and preparing a presentation, and listen to useful advice for the planning process. In preparation for their own classmate introductions, students complete a brainstorming map and listen to a model classmate introduction. They then learn useful tips for what to do before, during, and after a presentation and, finally, prepare and give brief classmate introductions in groups.

Lesson	Activities
Preparing to present	Doing a survey to get to know classmates; learning about the steps for a presentation
Introducing a classmate	Completing a brainstorming map; learning about the organization of a presentation; listening to a model classmate introduction
Presentation tips	An introduction to what good presenters do
My classmate introduction	Preparing and giving a classmate introduction

Preparing to present

1 Classmate interviews
Page 2

Warm-up

- Books closed. Tell students that in this course, they will give presentations in front of the class. This means that their classmates will be their audience. Explain that it is useful for students to know some information about the audience before giving a presentation, so that they can choose topics that match the audience's needs and interests. The tasks in this lesson will help students get to know their classmates' backgrounds, interests, and experiences.
- Tell students to look at the picture on page 2 in their Student's Books. Ask a few focusing questions about the picture. For example:
  Where do you think the people are?
  Do you think they know each other?
  What are they doing?

A

- Read the instructions aloud.
- Give students about one minute to think of information they'd like to find out about their classmates.

- Ask for a few volunteers to share their ideas with the class.

B

- Read the instructions aloud.
- Call on individual students to read the topics in the *Interview topic* column of the chart aloud.
- Point out the written example in the *Question* column of the chart.
- Give students about five minutes to add their own interview topic and complete the *Question* column.
- Explain that students will complete the remaining two columns in the chart when they do Exercise C.
- Walk around the classroom, helping students as necessary.

C

- Read the instructions aloud.
- Point out the written examples in the *Classmate* and *Answer* columns of the chart.
- Have students stand and give them about 10 minutes to complete the chart. Remind them to ask a different classmate each question and to write their names and answers in the last two columns of the chart.

Teaching tip For higher-level classes, tell students to ask each classmate one or two follow-up questions. For example:
A: *How many brothers and sisters do you have?*
B: *One brother and two sisters.*
A: *How old are they? What do they do?*

- Walk around the classroom, helping students as necessary.

Teaching tip If class time is limited, you may want to finish this activity when you notice that most students have four or five answers in the chart.

D

- Read the instructions aloud.
- Point out the model language to help students get started.
- Ask for a few volunteers to tell the class about two or three of their classmates.

② Presentation steps
Page 3

Notes

Useful language

to brainstorm to think of and write down a lot of ideas very quickly so that you can consider them carefully later

greeting saying hello or good morning / afternoon / evening to someone

to grow up to spend your childhood

outline a set of notes organized by main topics and details, written in preparation for a presentation

A

- Tell students they are now going to think about how to plan a presentation.
- Have students look at the pictures while you read the instructions aloud. Then call on individual students to read the steps written beneath each picture aloud.
- Give students about two minutes to number the steps in order. Point out that the first step (*Choose a presentation topic.*) has been numbered for them.
- Go over the answers with the whole class.

Answers

1. Choose a presentation topic.
2. Brainstorm.
3. Write an outline.
4. Make presentation notes.
5. Practice.

B 🔘 Track 2

- Read the instructions aloud. Then call on individual students to read Dan's advice aloud.
- Point out to students that the first step has been matched to the correct piece of advice.
- Give students about three minutes to match the rest of the steps to the advice. Then have them compare answers in pairs.
- Play the audio program and have students check their answers.
- Confirm answers by calling on individual students to read the advice and to say the matching step from Exercise A.

Answers

1. **Choose a presentation topic:** Think about your audience. Select something that will interest them.
2. **Brainstorm:** Write down as many topics and details as you can think of.
3. **Write an outline:** Organize the main topics and details.
4. **Make presentation notes:** Use note cards and write only brief phrases.
5. **Practice:** Go over your presentation notes out loud, and time your presentation.

Introducing a classmate

① Brainstorming
Page 4

Warm-up

- Books closed. Tell students they are now going to see how the *Presentation steps* on page 3 work. Draw the following brainstorming map on the board:

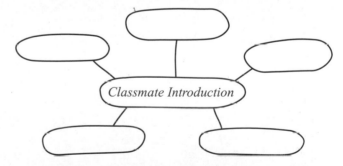

- Tell students to imagine that you are going to introduce one of their classmates to the class. Ask them to help you brainstorm some possible topics to include in your introduction. Elicit five or six topics from students (for example, the classmate's name, hometown, hobbies, job), and write them in the brainstorming map on the board, adding spaces to the map as needed.

- Now tell students that the classmate introduction will only be one to two minutes long, so you can't talk about all the topics. Ask them to help you choose three or four topics to include.
- Tell students that you now have a good start for an interesting, short classmate introduction. Explain that they will now look at Dan's brainstorming ideas.

A

- Tell students to open to page 4 in their Student's Books.
- Read the instructions aloud.
- Point out the example answer.
- Give students about two minutes to check the remaining topics. Then have them compare answers in pairs.
- Ask for volunteers to share their answers with the class.

Answers

Her hometown
A greeting and my classmate's name
A conclusion
Her family
Her free-time activities

B

- Read the instructions aloud. Then read the notes aloud.
- Make sure students understand that the notes are details that Dan brainstormed about each of the topics in his brainstorming map.
- Point out the example answer.
- Give students about two minutes to complete the brainstorming map.
- Read the main topics in the brainstorming map aloud one by one, and ask for volunteers to share the details they wrote.

Answers

Clockwise from top left:
Hi, my name is Dan.
introduce Emma
grew up in San Diego
small family, parents in Taipei
plays guitar
Thank you for listening.

② Organizing
Page 5

Notes

Useful language
however but

A

- Tell students that Dan has decided which topics and information to include in his classmate introduction presentation. Now he needs to organize the topics and details into the order he wants to talk about them.
- Read the instructions aloud.
- Read the bullet points and the model language aloud.

B Track 3

- Tell students they will have a chance to listen to Dan's presentation.
- Read the instructions aloud. Tell students to look at Exercise A to help them complete Dan's presentation.
- Point out the example answer.
- Give students about two minutes to read and complete the presentation. Then have them compare answers in pairs.
- Walk around the classroom, helping students as necessary.
- Play the audio program and have students check their answers.
- Write the correct answers on the board for students' reference.

Answers

name, introduce, going, tell, free-time, was, grew up, has, brother, free, know, Thank you

Presentation tips

Page 6

Notes

Useful language
gesture a physical action that expresses feelings, or that demonstrates size, shape, order, comparison, etc.
to make eye contact to look directly at another person's eyes
stress and emphasis using intonation, pitch, speed, or loudness to signal important information
tip a useful piece of advice
visual aid a poster, picture, slide, or chart used during a presentation to clarify or support the information being provided

Warm-up

- Books closed. Tell students that when they give a presentation, the content – *what* they say – is very important. Explain that it is also very important to pay attention to the delivery of the presentation – *how* they say it. Good presenters use posture, facial expressions, stress and emphasis, and gestures to get their message across and make their presentations clear and interesting.

Teaching tip As you say the above, you may want to demonstrate (or exaggerate) the aspects of delivery mentioned. You can deliberately use dramatic gestures, vary the speed, intonation, and loudness of your voice, and make eye contact with all the students.

A

- Tell students to open to page 6 in their Student's Books.
- Read the instructions aloud.
- Call on individual students to read the words and phrases in the box aloud. Then have them read the partial sentences silently. Explain any unfamiliar language.
- Point out the example answer.
- Give students about three minutes to complete the sentences. Then have them compare answers in pairs or small groups.
- Call on individual students to share their answers with the class.

Answers

1. Make eye contact
2. Relax
3. Use gestures
4. Smile and say "Thank you"
5. Practice
6. Use simple visual aids
7. Think about
8. Speak loudly and clearly
9. Make brief notes

B

- Explain to students that each of the presentation tips in Exercise A will be important to remember at different times in the process of planning and giving their presentations.
- Read the instructions aloud.
- Call on a student to read the first tip aloud. Then explain that eye contact is important *during* the presentation. Point out the example answer.
- Give students about three minutes to write their answers.
- Read each presentation tip aloud, and ask for volunteers to share their responses with the class.

Answers

1. D 2. B 3. D 4. A 5. B 6. D 7. A 8. D 9. B

C

- Tell students that the presentation tips in Exercise A will take time and practice to learn, and reassure them that they will not be expected to do all of them immediately.
- Have students form pairs.
- Read the instructions aloud.
- Point out the model language to help students get started.
- Give students about two minutes to talk about the tips.
- Ask for a few volunteers to share the presentation tips they chose, and to say why they chose them.
- Tell students they are now ready to prepare their own classmate introductions.

My classmate introduction

Page 7

A

- Read the description of the assignment in the box aloud. Then read the instructions aloud.
- Point out the sentence in the conclusion that is already in the brainstorming map.
- Have students find a classmate to interview, and give them time to ask and answer their questions. Remind students that they should take notes on their partners' answers because they will use that information when they complete their brainstorming maps.

Teaching tip If many of the students in your class know one another, you may want to encourage them to choose a classmate they don't know well. Alternatively, you can assign partners.

Teaching tip For lower-level classes, give students the option of including only two topics in their presentations. You may want to have students look back at the model brainstorming map on page 4 in their Student's Books for ideas.

Teaching tip For higher-level classes, encourage students to add one or two more topics and questions to their interview.

- Once students have interviewed their classmates, have them complete their brainstorming maps. If students need help, refer them to the model brainstorming map on page 4 in their Student's Books.
- Walk around the classroom, helping students as necessary.

B

Teaching tip Depending on your available class time, you may want to have students start this activity in class and finish it as homework.

- Read the instructions aloud.

- Give students time to complete their notes. Encourage them to write abbreviated notes rather than complete sentences, if possible.
- Walk around the classroom, helping students as necessary.

C

> **Teaching tip** If possible, bring some note cards or index cards to class for students to use for this first unit. Although using note cards is not introduced until Unit 1, it will be helpful for students to start the course using the correct materials.

- Read the instructions aloud.
- Explain that *final notes* are the notes that students will use during their presentations. Encourage students to make brief notes on note cards to speak from, and not to write out (or read) their entire presentations word for word. Give students time to transfer their notes onto note cards.
- Give students time to practice their presentations individually. Then have them practice in pairs. Encourage students to stand up, and remind them to use the presentation tips they chose in Exercise C on page 6.

D

- Have students form groups of three or four.
- Read the instructions aloud.
- Have groups decide in what order students will give their presentations. Tell them that they should stand up when it is their turn.
- Walk around the classroom, listening in to as many groups as possible.

> **Teaching tip** At this stage, it is not necessary to evaluate students' presentations. However, if you notice that many students need more practice with certain skills, for example, eye contact or speaking clearly, you can address those issues with the whole class when all students have finished their presentations.

1 A motto for life

Overview

In this unit, students talk about personal mottoes and what they mean. They talk about how personal values relate to different mottoes. In preparation for their own presentations about a personal motto, students look at brainstorming notes, complete a presentation outline, and listen to a model presentation about a personal motto. They then practice writing and using presentation notes and, finally, prepare and give their own presentations about a personal motto.

Lesson	Activities
Topic focus	Discussing people's mottoes; talking about personal values
Language focus	Explaining the meaning of a motto; relating a motto to a past experience
Organization focus	Focusing on brainstorming ideas and creating an outline for a presentation about a personal motto
Presentation focus	Focusing on the introduction, body, and conclusion of a presentation; listening to a model presentation about a personal motto: *Words to Live By*
Presentation skills focus	Making and using presentation notes; making eye contact when speaking
Present yourself!	Brainstorming ideas; creating an outline; giving a presentation about a personal motto

Topic focus

1 This is me.
Page 8

> **Notes**
>
> **Useful language**
> **to count** to have value or importance
> **to enrich** to improve the quality of something by adding something else
> **to leap** to make a large jump
> **material thing** a physical object
> **motto** a word or phrase that expresses a belief
> **sense of humor** the ability to be amused by something you see, hear, or think about

Warm-up
- To help explain the idea of personal mottoes, if possible, you may want to elicit one or two mottoes or sayings in the students' own language. It may also help to ask students if any English mottoes they know can be translated into their language.
- Ask students if they or their friends have a personal motto. Elicit one or two from them and ask them to try to explain them. If no one has a motto, write one on the board and tell students that this is your motto. Try to elicit what the motto means. Write any other mottoes that students know on the board and try to elicit their meanings.
- Tell students that in this unit, they will learn some mottoes in English and think about their own personal mottoes.

A
- Have students form pairs and tell them to open to page 8 in their Student's Books.
- Read the instructions aloud.
- Read the mottoes aloud, and explain any unfamiliar language.
- Give pairs about two minutes to discuss what they think the mottoes mean.
- Walk around the classroom, helping students as necessary.

- Call on a few students to share their interpretations of the mottoes.

B

- Read the instructions aloud.
- Call on individual students to read the sentences aloud. Explain any unfamiliar language.
- Point out the example answer.
- Give students about three minutes to match the mottoes to the sentences.
- Have students compare answers in pairs before you go over the answers with the whole class.

Answers

1. A sense of humor can make you feel better.
2. Don't give up too easily.
3. You should try to enjoy each day of your life.
4. Simple things in life make us happy, not material things.
5. Experiencing things with others enriches your life.
6. You should consider a situation carefully before acting.

C

- Read the instructions aloud.
- Point out the model language to help students get started.
- Ask for a few volunteers to share their responses with the class. Encourage students to give reasons for their choices.

> **Teaching tip** If time allows, take a class poll to find out which sentences in Exercise B were chosen by the most students. Lead a brief class discussion about the most popular sentences and how students' choices relate to their personal values.

2 My personal values
Page 9

Notes

Useful language

to aim to plan for a specific purpose

improbable surprising or not likely to happen

rehearsal a practice session

personal value a belief about what is right and wrong, and what is important in life

to shape to influence something, especially a belief or an idea

to value to believe something is very important

A

- Elicit an explanation of *personal values* (see *Notes* above).
- Tell students they will now have a chance to think about their own personal values. If necessary, explain how mottoes can relate to personal values.

- Read the instructions aloud.
- Ask for volunteers to read the *Personal values* in the box aloud. Explain any unfamiliar language.
- Call on a student to read the model language aloud.
- Have students form pairs.
- Give pairs about three minutes to discuss their personal values. Remind them to explain why the values are important to them.
- Walk around the classroom, helping students as necessary.
- Ask for a few volunteers to share their responses with the class.

B

- Have students stay in their pairs from Exercise A.
- Read the instructions aloud.
- Call on individual students to read the mottoes aloud. Explain any unfamiliar language.
- Point out the example answer.
- Give pairs about five minutes to match the *Personal values* from the box in Exercise A to the mottoes.
- Walk around the classroom, helping students as necessary.
- Have pairs compare answers before you go over the answers with the whole class.

Answers

Life is not a rehearsal: enjoying life

Never stop learning: getting an education

Always do what you are afraid to do: taking risks

Money makes the world go around: valuing money

A smile can brighten someone's darkest day: being kind to others

Make new friends but keep the old. One is silver, and the other is gold: keeping good relationships

Aim for the impossible, and you'll achieve the improbable: following dreams

Choose a job you love, and you'll never have to work a day in your life: enjoying your work

C

- Read the instructions aloud.
- Give students about two minutes to choose a motto and write the personal value that shapes it. Make sure students understand that they can choose any motto from Exercise A on page 8 or Exercise B on page 9.
- Walk around the classroom, helping students as necessary.

D

- Read the instructions aloud.
- Call on a student to read the model language above the chart aloud.
- Point out the written example in the chart.
- Have students stand and give them about five minutes to interview two classmates and complete the chart.
- When students have completed their interviews and returned to their seats, point out the model language at

the bottom of the page. Then ask for a few volunteers to share the information about their classmates with the class.

Language focus

① Mottoes and their meanings
Page 10

Notes

Useful language

to define to explain the meaning of something

effective producing the intended results

to paraphrase to use different words to say the same thing

spice a flavor enhancer for food; in this case, something that adds interest or excitement

variety an assortment of different things

A 💿 Track 4

- Have students look at the pictures while you read the instructions aloud.
- Ask for volunteers to read the answer choices below the pictures aloud.
- Point out the example answer.
- Play the audio program once or twice as needed.
- Check answers by calling on individual students to share their responses with the class.

Answers

1. **Josh:** following dreams
2. **Yumi:** enjoying life
3. **Andy:** taking risks

B 💿 Track 4

- Read the instructions aloud.
- Give students about one minute to read the information in the chart.
- Point out the example answers.
- Play the audio program once or twice as needed.
- Have students compare answers in pairs before you go over the answers with the whole class.

Teaching tip If time allows, have students discuss which of the three mottoes they agree with the most and why.

Answers

1. **Josh:** Life; control
2. **Yumi:** spice; interesting
3. **Andy:** don't, mistakes; important

C

- Have students form pairs.
- Read the instructions aloud.
- Read the language in the box aloud, and have students repeat it. Encourage students to use this language when they do the activity.
- Give students about two minutes to choose their mottoes and to think about how to explain them. When students are ready, point out the model language to help them get started.
- Give pairs about three minutes to discuss their mottoes.
- Walk around the classroom, helping students as necessary.
- Ask for a few volunteers to share their answers with the class.

② Mottoes and experiences
Page 11

Notes

Useful language

entrance exam a test taken in order to enter a particular high school or university

A 💿 Track 5

- Read the instructions aloud.
- Ask for volunteers to read the answer choices aloud. Explain (or have students explain to their classmates) any unfamiliar language.
- Play the audio program once or twice as needed.
- Have students compare answers in pairs before you go over the answers with the whole class.

Answers

1. **Josh:** failed an entrance exam
2. **Yumi:** started university
3. **Andy:** was asked to join a band

B 💿 Track 5

- Read the instructions aloud.
- Give students time to read the answer choices. Explain any unfamiliar language.
- Point out the example answer.
- Play the audio program once or twice as needed.
- Ask for volunteers to share their answers with the class.

Answers

1. **Josh:** (1) focused on weak areas, (2) took extra classes, (3) did practice exams
2. **Yumi:** (1) made a list, (2) got information, (3) met managers
3. **Andy:** (1) learned from his mistakes, (2) practiced even more, (3) started singing

❸ My life experiences
Page 11

Notes

Useful language

disappointed unhappy or discouraged because of a
  bad result
to rely on to depend on or trust

A

- Tell students that most mottoes come from situations or experiences from which people have learned important life lessons. Ask students to think about examples of those kinds of experiences in their own lives. Elicit examples from a few volunteers.
- Read the instructions aloud.
- Point out the written example.
- Give students about five minutes to write about their own experience.
- Walk around the classroom, helping students as necessary.

B

- Have students form groups of three or four.
- Read the instructions aloud.
- Read the language in the box aloud, and have students repeat it. Encourage students to use this language when they do the activity.
- Point out the model language to help students get started.

> **Teaching tip** For lower-level classes, you may want to give one or two extra examples of mottoes and their related experiences before students work in groups.

- Give groups about five minutes to share their mottoes and experiences.
- Walk around the classroom, helping students as necessary.
- Ask for a few volunteers to share their mottoes and experiences with the class.

Organization focus

❶ Tim's motto
Page 12

> **Teaching tip** As this is the first full unit students will do, you may want to spend some time orienting students to the next lesson. Explain that the activities are designed to guide students through the process of preparing and organizing their own presentations about a personal motto, which they will do at the end of the unit.

Notes

Useful language

preview advance information about something
to relate (to) to be connected to
to remind to make someone aware of something they
  have forgotten

A

- Explain to students that Tim is a student in a presentation course. He is going to give a presentation about his personal motto.
- Have students look at the picture on page 12 in their Student's Books, but have them cover Exercises B and C and page 13. Tell them to look only at the picture while you read the instructions and questions aloud.
- Elicit a few responses to the questions.

> **Possible answers**
>
> His personal values are being kind to others and keeping good relationships.
> He found someone's bag and returned it.

- Tell students they are going to find out more information about Tim's motto in this lesson and in the next lesson of the unit.

B

- Have students uncover their books.

> **Teaching tip** Before doing Exercises B and C, you may want to give a brief introduction to the outline on page 13 of the Student's Book. Explain the following:
> - Presentations are usually organized into three parts: an introduction, a body, and a conclusion.
> - In an outline, the main topics are represented by capital letters: *A*, *B*, *C*, etc.
> - Smaller points, or details, are represented by numbers: *1*, *2*, *3*, etc.

- Read the instructions aloud.
- Have students look at the brainstorming map and at the outline on page 13.
- Give students about two minutes to check the eight topics included in the outline.
- Ask for volunteers to say the topics they checked.

> **Answers**
>
> **Clockwise from top:**
> How my motto helps me in life
> My personal values
> The meaning
> My motto
> A statement to connect with the audience
> A wish for the audience that relates to my motto
> A preview of the presentation
> Past experiences that relate to my motto

c

> **Teaching tip** You may want to have students do this exercise in pairs, so they can help each other and share ideas.

- Read the instructions aloud.
- Give students time to read the notes. Explain any unfamiliar language.
- Give students about three minutes to complete the outline.
- Walk around the classroom, helping students as necessary.
- If students have been working individually, have them work in pairs to compare their answers.

② Tim's outline 💿 Track 6
Page 13

> **Notes**
>
> **Useful language**
> **to appreciate** to understand the value of something

- Read the instructions aloud.
- Play the audio program and have students follow along with the outline.
- Check answers by reading through the outline aloud and calling on individual students to say the missing information.

> **Answers**
>
> I. B. 2. honesty
> I. C. 3. how my motto helps me in life
> II. B. 2. doesn't take a lot of effort to be kind to others
> II. C. 1. found bag in park, returned it to hotel
> III. A. 3. reminds me I can make the world a better place

Presentation focus

① Introduction
Pages 14 and 15

> **Teaching tip** Before doing this lesson, you may want to encourage students to review the vocabulary and language presented in Unit 1. Hand out a copy of the Unit 1 **Language summary** (Teacher's Manual page 52) to each student in the class. Alternatively, refer students to the appropriate sections in their Student's Books if they need help completing the tasks.

- Tell students they are now going to focus on each section of Tim's presentation separately.
- Elicit the names of the three parts of a presentation: the introduction, the body, and the conclusion.

- Read the instructions aloud.
- Read the bullet points and the model language aloud. Let students know that the missing words in the presentation can all be found on pages 10 to 13.
- Give students about two minutes to read and complete the introduction.
- Walk around the classroom, helping students as necessary.

② Body
Pages 14 and 15

> **Notes**
>
> **Useful language**
> **to accept** to agree to take
> **panic** a feeling of strong anxiety or fear
> **reward** a prize (often money) given to someone in exchange for a kind act
> **staff** a group of people who work for an organization
> **valuables** expensive or important possessions

- Read the instructions aloud.
- Call on a student to read the bullet points aloud. If necessary, remind students that the missing words can all be found on pages 10 to 13.
- Give students about three minutes to read and complete the body.
- Walk around the classroom, helping students as necessary.

③ Conclusion
Pages 14 and 15

- Read the instructions aloud.
- Call on a student to read the bullet points and the model language aloud. If necessary, remind students that the missing words can all be found on pages 10 to 13.
- Give students about two minutes to read and complete the conclusion.
- Walk around the classroom, helping students as necessary.

④ Tim's presentation 💿 Track 6
Pages 14 and 15

- Read the instructions aloud.
- Play the audio program and have students check their answers.
- Write the correct answers on the board for students' reference.

> **Answers**
>
> **Introduction:** feel, family, motto, experiences, helps
> **Body:** other, means, motto, bag
> **Conclusion:** appreciate, honest, better

Teaching tip You may want to finish by having students talk about their own experiences when they helped someone, or when someone was kind to them. Write questions on the board, and have students discuss them in pairs or small groups. For example:
When was the last time you helped someone? What did you do? How did it make you feel?
Has a stranger ever been kind to you? What happened? How did you feel?
Have you ever lost something valuable? What happened?

Presentation skills focus

① Presentation notes
Page 16

Notes

Useful language

to apply to request something by completing a form (see *Usage tip* below)
to hire to employ or pay someone to do a job
internship a period of training for a job

Usage tip
apply
People apply *to* a company (or a person or department) *for* a job.

- Read the information at the top of the page aloud.
- Read the instructions aloud.
- Give students time to look at each picture and read the *do* or *don't* below it. Explain any unfamiliar language.
- Call on individual students to read each of the *dos* and *don'ts* aloud. For each *don't*, explain that this is an example of what *not* to do when making or using note cards. For each *do*, explain that this shows what students *should* do when making or using note cards.
- Ask for a volunteer to read the presentation tip aloud.

Teaching tip You may want to model the presentation tip by holding up the Student's Book and speaking from one of the note cards, pausing a few times to make eye contact with the class. Alternatively, you could look at your note cards as you speak to illustrate what *not* to do.

② Your turn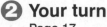
Page 17

Notes

Useful language

homestay a period of time spent living in someone else's home, usually for educational purposes in another country
nervous worried or anxious

A
- Read the instructions aloud.
- Point out the example answer.
- Give students about two minutes to read the example passage and complete the note cards. Make sure students understand that they need to complete the note cards with short phrases and not full sentences.
- Walk around the classroom, helping students as necessary.
- Ask for volunteers to write the answers on the board.
- Go over the answers with the whole class. Make any necessary corrections to the answers on the board.

Answers
- Motto: **Just jump**
- Meaning
  don't **think** too **much before doing** something
  take **action when you** have opportunity
- Experience
  a **year** ago, had **chance to do** homestay in U.K.
  nervous, but decided **to go**
  best experience of my **life**

B
- Have students form pairs.
- Read the instructions aloud.
- Model the task by standing in front of the class and covering the example passage with a piece of paper. Begin the presentation using the model language below the instructions. Remember to demonstrate the presentation tip by looking up when you speak.
- Give pairs about five minutes to practice giving the presentation. Have students stand and remind them to make eye contact with the audience.
- Walk around the classroom, helping students as necessary.

C
- Read the instructions aloud.
- Point out the written example.
- Give students about three minutes to choose their mottoes and make notes. Tell students that they may choose any of the mottoes from Unit 1 or other ones they like.
- Walk around the classroom, helping students as necessary.

D

- Have students form pairs.
- Read the instructions aloud.
- Point out the model language to help students get started.
- Give pairs about five minutes to present their mottoes. Have students stand, and remind them to make eye contact with the audience as they speak.
- When students finish, tell them that they are now ready to begin planning their own presentations about a personal motto.

Present yourself!

❶ Brainstorming
Page 18

> **Teaching tip** As this is the first presentation students will do, you may want to go over the next two pages and have them begin the planning process in class, so that you can be available to answer any questions they may have.

- Read the assignment in the box at the top of the page aloud.
- Read the instructions aloud.
- Give students time to choose a motto. If they need help doing this, refer them to pages 8 to 11 in their Student's Books for ideas.
- Have students complete the brainstorming map. Remind them not to write complete sentences. They should brainstorm as much information as possible about their mottoes and make brief notes.
- Walk around the classroom, helping students as necessary.
- If students need help, refer them to the example brainstorming map on page 12 (Exercise B) in their Student's Books. Alternatively, have students watch while you draw a brainstorming map with notes about a motto of yours on the board. Then review the brainstorming map with the students.

❷ Organizing
Page 19

> **Teaching tip** Depending on your available class time, you may want to have students start this activity in class and finish it as homework.

- Read the instructions aloud.
- Have students read the topics in the outline.
- Review the outline format, explaining that students should write the details from their brainstorming maps under the appropriate main topics.

- Give students time to think of a presentation title and complete the outline.
- Walk around the classroom, helping students as necessary.

> **Teaching tip** If students need more help organizing their outlines, you may want to collect the outlines and give written feedback on them to the students.

- Have students make their final notes on note cards. Remind them that they should speak from abbreviated notes written on note cards, and should not read out their presentations word for word.
- Remind students to practice their presentations.

> **Teaching tip** If time allows, you may want to have students form pairs or groups and take turns practicing their presentations in class. Suggest that students ask a classmate to time the length of their presentations, and encourage them to make suggestions to help improve their classmates' presentations.

❸ Presenting
Page 19

> **Teaching tip** Depending on your class size, you will need to determine the best format (group or whole class) and time limit for students' presentations.

- Read the instructions aloud.
- Explain the format and time limit for students' presentations (see *Teaching tip* above). Make sure students understand that they will be expected to use the language and presentation skills they learned in Unit 1.
- If you plan to have students use the **Outline worksheet** and **Peer evaluation form**, or if you plan to use the **Assessment form** during students' presentations, be sure to make the appropriate number of copies before students begin their presentations.
- When students finish their presentations, have them complete the **Self-evaluation** on page 80 in their Student's Books.

Unit 1	Teacher's Manual page
Language summary	52
Outline worksheet	58
Peer evaluation form	64
Assessment form	65

2 Young people today

Overview

In this unit, students talk about survey topics and survey their classmates. They practice describing the aims, survey group, and results of a survey. In preparation for their own survey presentations, students brainstorm survey questions, complete a presentation outline, and listen to a model presentation about a youth survey. They then practice explaining visual aids and, finally, conduct their own surveys and present their results to the class.

Lesson	Activities
Topic focus	Talking about survey topics, questions, and results; surveying classmates
Language focus	Describing a survey; reporting survey results
Organization focus	Focusing on brainstorming ideas and creating an outline for a survey presentation
Presentation focus	Focusing on the introduction, body, and conclusion of a presentation; listening to a model survey presentation: *Young People's Eating Habits*
Presentation skills focus	Explaining visual aids; using visual aids effectively
Present yourself!	Brainstorming questions and doing a survey; creating an outline; giving a presentation about the survey results

Topic focus

1 Survey questions
Page 20

Notes

Useful language

attitude an opinion or a feeling about an issue or a topic

challenging difficult

lecture series an event at which several speakers give talks about a certain topic

to make a difference to change a situation for the better

one-third one of three equal parts; 33 percent

researcher a person who studies a certain topic in order to learn more about it

Culture tip

Cultural comparison

This unit provides many opportunities to have students discuss how their own culture is similar to or different from other cultures. When possible, encourage students to discuss the survey results presented in the unit activities, and compare them with what they think the results would be in their own culture.

Warm-up

- Books closed. Tell students to imagine that they are professors or researchers. They are going to give presentations about important issues that affect young people today.
- Have students brainstorm topics related to young people's lifestyles, behavior, beliefs, and values. Write their ideas on the board.
- Ask students how they would find out information about young people for their lectures. Try to elicit the notion of conducting a survey.

A

- Tell students to open to page 20 in their Student's Books.
- Read the instructions aloud.
- Give students time to read the announcement silently. Explain any unfamiliar language.
- Ask for a few volunteers to share their responses with the class.
- To finish, ask students if they think the survey results in the announcement would be similar or different for young people in their country.

B

- Read the instructions aloud.
- Read the questions aloud and have students repeat them. Explain any unfamiliar language.
- Have students look back at Exercise A. Point out the example answer to them.
- Have students work alone or in pairs to match the questions to the survey results.
- Walk around the classroom, helping students as necessary.
- Go over the answers with the whole class.

Answers

a: Half of all young people believe they can make a difference in the world.

b: Only 10 percent of young people say they study over an hour a day.

c: Two-thirds of teens say friends are very important in their lives.

d: Forty percent of 18-year-olds say they go shopping every weekend.

e: Most teens say they receive over $100 a month from their parents.

f: One-third of all high school students think that school is not challenging.

C

- Read the instructions aloud.
- Encourage students to think of different topics from the ones they brainstormed on the board in the *Warm-up*, if possible.
- Point out the model language to help students get started.
- Elicit responses from a few students and add the topics to the list on the board.

❷ Youth survey
Page 21

Notes

Useful language

to browse the Internet to look at various Web sites
feature a characteristic or part

Usage tip

cell phone
Cell phones can also be called *mobile phones.*

A

- Read the instructions aloud.
- Call on individual students to read the survey topics and questions in the chart aloud. Point out that the questions are all *Wh-* questions.

- Give students about five minutes to complete the chart. Encourage students to add a topic that really interests them.
- Walk around the classroom, helping students as necessary.
- Ask for a few volunteers to share the topics and questions they wrote.

B

- Tell students they will now have a chance to conduct a brief survey of their classmates.
- Read the instructions aloud.
- Point out the written example in the chart.
- Tell students to write their own topics from Exercise A (number 4) in the chart.
- Read the model language aloud with a student.
- Have students stand and give them about 10 minutes to survey 3 classmates and write their answers in the chart.
- Walk around the classroom, helping students as necessary.

C

- Have students form pairs.
- Read the instructions aloud.
- Point out the model language to help students get started.
- Give pairs about five minutes to share their survey results.
- Ask for a few volunteers to share their results with the class.

Language focus

1 Describing a survey
Page 22

Notes

Useful language

career a job for which you are trained and in which you can advance during your working life

to conduct to organize and direct

gender being either male or female

preference something that you like better than other things

range the level to which something is limited

Usage tip

conduct a survey

This means the same as *do a survey* but is more formal.

Warm-up

- Books closed. Write on the board the following information: *Survey topic: Interests and hobbies; Results: 30% = tennis and swimming; 15% = reading magazines; 23% = listening to music.*
- Tell students that these are the results of a survey you did about interests and hobbies.
- Explain to students that the details about the group of people in a survey are very important. Tell students to think about questions they could ask someone about their survey group. Try to elicit from students the following questions:
  How many people did you ask?
  Who did you ask?
  How old were the people?
  How many males and females did you ask?
- Once you have elicited these questions (or given students these questions), tell students that in this lesson they are going to practice fully describing the aims, survey group, and results of a survey.

A ◯ Track 7

- Tell students to open to page 22 in their Student's Books and look at the pictures.
- Ask for volunteers to read the topics below the pictures aloud. Explain any unfamiliar language.
- Read the instructions aloud. Encourage students to listen for key words that will help them choose the correct topics.
- Play the audio program once or twice as needed.
- Check answers by calling on individual students to name topic numbers 1, 2, and 3.

Answers

1. **Sun Hee:** TV-viewing habits
2. **Ken:** Exercise habits
3. **Paula:** News preferences

B ◯ Track 7

- Read the instructions aloud.
- Give students time to read the information in the chart. Explain any unfamiliar language.
- Play the audio program once or twice as needed.
- Have students compare answers in pairs before you go over the answers with the whole class.

Answers

1. **Sun Hee:** 16 teenagers, 15 to 19, 9 girls / 7 boys
2. **Ken:** 19 young adults, 18 to 24, 10 men / 9 women
3. **Paula:** 12 university students, 18 to 22, 6 males / 6 females

C

- Tell students that they are now going to play the roles of the three speakers in Exercises A and B: Sun Hee, Ken, and Paula.
- Have students form pairs.
- Read the instructions aloud.
- Read the language in the box aloud, and have students repeat it. Encourage students to use this language when they do the activity.
- To model the task, call on a student to read the model language aloud, completing it with the appropriate information from *Sun Hee* in Exercise B.
- Give students about five minutes to do the role play.
- Walk around the classroom, helping students as necessary.
- Ask for a few volunteers to describe the surveys to the class.

2 Survey results
Page 23

Notes

Useful language

one-quarter one of four equal parts of something; 25 percent

percentage a number showing the amount out of a total of one hundred

Grammar tip

Fractions and percentages

Fractions and percentages are followed by the preposition *of*. For example:
One-third *of* high school students don't have cell phones.
Forty percent *of* university students live with their parents.

Usage tip

Saying fractions

People often say *a third* instead of *one-third*. *One-quarter* can be said as *a quarter*, *a fourth*, or *one-fourth*. People often just say *half* instead of *one-half*.

A ⊙ Track 8

- Read the instructions aloud.
- Tell students to look at the results and to notice how the numbers are represented differently. Try to elicit that there are three types of results: fractions (one-third), percentages (28 percent), and whole numbers (one out of five). Explain that survey results are often expressed in these three ways. Ask students how they would represent 50 percent as a fraction (one-half) and as a whole number (one out of two).
- Play the audio program once or twice as needed.
- Have students compare answers in pairs before you go over the answers with the whole class.

Answers

1. **Sun Hee:** 47%, one-third, 20%, one out of five
2. **Ken:** 28%, 45%, one-quarter, 2%
3. **Paula:** 20%, 3%, 10%, two-thirds

B ⊙ Track 8

- Have students look at the visual aids while you explain that the three speakers used them to help show their survey results to the audience.
- Read the instructions aloud. Make sure students understand that they should write all of the numbers as percentages.
- Point out the two example answers.
- Play the audio program once or twice as needed.
- Go over the answers with the whole class.

Answers

1. **Sun Hee:** 0–9: 20%, 10–19: 33%, 20 or more: 47%
2. **Ken:** every day: 28%, a few times a week: 45%, once a week: 25%, less than once a week: 2%
3. **Paula:** newspaper: 20%, radio: 3%, TV: 10%, Internet: 67%

❸ My class survey
Page 23

Notes

Useful language

fraction a number that represents parts of a whole number, for example, one-half (½) or one-quarter (¼)

transportation the ways people travel from one place to another

A

- Read the instructions aloud.
- Give students about five minutes to choose a topic and write their survey question.
- Walk around the classroom, helping students as necessary.

- Have students stand and give them about 10 minutes to interview their classmates. Remind them that they should write down their classmates' answers because they will need that information when they do Exercise B.

Teaching tip You may want to tell students how many classmates they should interview. A limit of about six to eight classmates will provide a good variety of responses and will allow students to calculate the results in Exercise B. Ideally, each student will ask the same number of classmates.

B

- Read the instructions aloud.
- Read the language in the box aloud, and have students repeat it. Encourage students to use this language when they do the activity.
- Give students time to organize and calculate their data. Encourage them to use different ways of representing the numbers.
- Point out the model language to help students get started.
- Ask for a few volunteers to report their survey results to the class. Alternatively, have students share their results in small groups.
- To finish, ask students which survey results surprised them.

Organization focus

❶ Hannah's youth survey
Page 24

Notes

Useful language

junk food unhealthy food containing a lot of sugar or fat

official a person who is in a position of authority

recommendation a suggestion

summary a brief statement giving the important facts about something

A

- Tell students to open to page 24 in their Student's Books, but have them cover Exercises B and C and page 25. Tell them to look only at the picture while you read the instructions and questions aloud.
- Elicit a few responses to the questions.

Possible answers

The survey topic is eating habits / preferences.
The results were that young people don't eat enough healthy food / eat too much junk food.

- Tell students they are going to find out more information about Hannah's survey in this lesson and in the next lesson of the unit.

B

- Have students uncover their books.
- Read the instructions aloud.
- Have students look at the brainstorming notes and at the outline on page 25.
- Point out that Hannah's brainstorming notes are in a simple list form rather than in a brainstorming map (like the one in Unit 1 on page 12 in their Student's Books). Explain that students will have a chance to practice different types of brainstorming notes, so they can decide which style is most comfortable for them.
- Give students about two minutes to check the eight topics included in the outline.
- Ask for volunteers to say the topics they checked.

Answers

A summary of the results

A description of the survey group

A question about healthy foods

General information about the topic

The aim of the survey

My conclusion and recommendation

A question about eating habits and how healthy they think they are

A question about junk food and fast food

C

Teaching tip You may want to have students do this exercise in pairs, so they can help each other and share ideas.

- Read the instructions aloud.
- Give students time to read the notes. Explain any unfamiliar language.
- Give students about three minutes to complete the outline.
- Walk around the classroom, helping students as necessary.
- If students have been working individually, have them compare their answers in pairs.

2 Hannah's outline 💿 Track 9
Page 25

- Read the instructions aloud.
- Play the audio program and have students follow along with the outline.
- Check answers by reading through the outline aloud and calling on individual students to say the missing information.

Answers

I.   A. 2. young people buying more fast food than ever

I.   B. find out about university students' eating habits

II. A. 2. group included 11 women, 7 men

II. B. 2. 25 percent, pretty healthy

II. C. 2. one-third eat vegetables every day

II. D. 2. 75 percent eat fast food at least once a week

III. B. 2. University officials should make more healthy foods available.

Presentation focus

1 Introduction
Pages 26 and 27

Teaching tip Before doing this lesson, you may want to encourage students to review the vocabulary and language presented in Unit 2. Hand out a copy of the Unit 2 **Language summary** (Teacher's Manual page 53) to each student in the class. Alternatively, refer students to the appropriate sections in their Student's Books if they need help completing the tasks.

Notes

Useful language

expert a person who has a high level of skill or knowledge about something

---

- Tell students they are now going to focus on each section of Hannah's presentation separately.
- Read the instructions aloud.
- Read the bullet points and the model language aloud. If necessary, remind students that the missing words in the presentation can all be found on pages 22 to 25.
- Give students about two minutes to read and complete the introduction.
- Walk around the classroom, helping students as necessary.

2 Body
Pages 26 and 27

Notes

Useful language

chart a way of representing information by putting it into vertical rows and boxes on paper

graph a drawing of lines or bars that show how different amounts are related

to illustrate to show

table a set of facts or numbers arranged in rows and columns on a page

---

- Read the instructions aloud.
- Call on a student to read the bullet points aloud.
- Give students about three minutes to read and complete the body.
- Walk around the classroom, helping students as necessary.

❸ Conclusion
Pages 26 and 27

Notes

Useful language

to conclude to reach a decision or an opinion after taking various facts into consideration (see *Usage tip* below)

Usage tip

conclusion / to conclude

Students have learned that the *conclusion* is the end of a presentation. This unit expands its use to include the definition given above.

- Read the instructions aloud.
- Call on a student to read the bullet points and the model language aloud.
- Give students about two minutes to read and complete the conclusion.
- Walk around the classroom, helping students as necessary.

❹ Hannah's presentation 💿 Track 9
Pages 26 and 27

- Read the instructions aloud.
- Play the audio program and have students check their answers.
- Write the correct answers on the board for students' reference.

Answers

Introduction: habits, fast, find

Body: interviewed, included, pretty, one-third, surveyed, once

Conclusion: eating, students, officials

Teaching tip You may want to finish by having students discuss their reactions to Hannah's survey results. Write questions on the board, and have students discuss them in pairs or small groups. For example:
Which of Hannah's results surprised you the most? Which ones did not surprise you?
Do you think the eating habits of young people in your country are similar or different? In what ways?

Presentation skills focus

❶ Explaining visual aids
Page 28

Notes

Useful language

attractive pleasant to look at

informative containing interesting, relevant information; educational

Venn diagram a drawing of connected circles that shows how different amounts are related

Usage tip

Referring to visual aids

In PowerPoint presentations, the term *slide* is often used to refer to graphs, tables, and charts.

Venn diagram

In speech, Venn diagrams are often referred to simply as *diagrams*.

Warm-up

- Books closed. Ask students to think back to Hannah's presentation about young people's eating habits. Elicit some of the facts and information students remember from the presentation. Ask students if they remember how Hannah showed the audience the information. If necessary, have students open to page 27 in their Student's Books and look again at the presentation.
- Elicit that she not only told the audience the information verbally, but also used visual aids (graphs, tables, and charts).
- Tell students that using visual aids to present survey results can help the audience remember specific information such as numbers, and it can help presenters remember the information they want to give. In addition, using visual aids is one way to make a presentation with lots of facts and numbers more interesting.

A

- Have students form pairs.
- Tell students to open to page 28 in their Student's Books.
- Read the information at the top of the page aloud.
- Read the instructions aloud.
- Give pairs about two minutes to talk about the information in each visual aid.
- Ask for a few volunteers to share their responses with the class.

Possible answers

1. The countries where university students want to study English
2. The kind of music young people prefer
3. The ways people watch movies at home
4. The popular weekend activities for students

B 🔘 Track 10

- Read the instructions aloud.
- Play the audio program once or twice as needed.
- Have students compare answers in their pairs from Exercise A before you go over the answers with the whole class.

Answers

1. graph   2. pie chart   3. Venn diagram   4. table

- Ask for a volunteer to read the presentation tip aloud.

② Your turn
Page 29

A

- Read the instructions aloud.
- Read the language in the box aloud, and have students repeat it.
- Give students about five minutes to write their sentences.
- Walk around the classroom, helping students as necessary.

Possible answers

1. As this graph shows, one-third of university students said they want to study English in the U.K.
2. As this pie chart explains, 45 percent of young people said they prefer hip hop music.
3. As this Venn diagram makes clear, 40 percent of people said they watch movies on TV or DVD.
4. As this table illustrates, 1 in 10 teens said they shop on weekends.

B

- Have students form groups of three or four.
- Read the instructions aloud.
- Point out the model language to help students get started.
- Give groups about five minutes to share their sentences. Remind them to use different expressions for the numbers when possible. Have students stand and encourage them to hold a notebook or textbook up and, imagining it's a visual aid, practice pointing to it as they say their sentences.
- Walk around the classroom, helping students as necessary.

C

- Read the instructions aloud.
- Give students about 10 minutes to create their visual aids. Remind them to follow the presentation tip on page 28.
- Walk around the classroom, helping students as necessary.

D

- Have students form pairs.
- Read the instructions aloud.
- Give students about two minutes to practice individually. Then have them stand and take turns presenting their visual aids. Encourage them to also use the presentation skills they learned in Unit 1 (for example, making eye contact with the audience).
- Call on a few students to present their visual aids to the class.
- When students finish, tell them that they are now ready to begin planning their own survey presentations.

Present yourself!

① Brainstorming
Page 30

A

- Read the assignment in the box at the top of the page aloud.
- Read the instructions aloud.
- Give students time to choose a survey topic. If they need help with this, refer them to pages 20 to 22 in their Student's Books for ideas.
- Have students brainstorm their survey questions. Refer them to the *Example survey questions* in the brainstorming map.
- Walk around the classroom, helping students as necessary.

B

- Read the instructions aloud.
- Give students time to complete their interviews.

> **Teaching tip** As the survey activity may take some time, you may want to assign the interviews as homework. If you choose to do so, you can encourage students to interview people other than their classmates.

- Remind students to take careful notes on people's answers to their survey questions.

② Organizing
Page 31

> **Teaching tip** Depending on your available class time, you may want to have students start this activity in class and finish it as homework.

- Read the instructions aloud.
- Have students read the topics in the outline.
- If necessary, review the outline format, explaining that students should write the details from their research and their interview notes under the appropriate main topics.

- Give students time to think of a presentation title and complete the outline.
- Walk around the classroom, helping students as necessary.

> **Teaching tip** If students need more help organizing their outlines, you may want to collect the outlines and give written feedback on them to the students.

- Have students make their final notes on note cards. Remind them that they should speak from abbreviated notes written on note cards, and should not read out their presentations word for word.
- Remind students to practice their presentations.

> **Teaching tip** If time allows, you may want to have students form pairs or groups and take turns practicing their presentations in class. Suggest that students ask a classmate to time the length of their presentations, and encourage them to make suggestions to help improve their classmates' presentations.

❸ Presenting
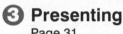
Page 31

> **Teaching tip** Depending on your class size, you will need to determine the best format (group or whole class) and time limit for students' presentations.

> **Teaching tip** Students may require additional planning time and/or resources to create their visual aids. If possible, allow some time for students to work on them in class and provide supplies such as poster paper and markers.

- Read the instructions aloud.
- Explain the format and time limit for students' presentations (see *Teaching tip* on the left). Make sure students understand that they will be expected to use the language and presentation skills they learned in Unit 2, as well any appropriate language and skills they learned in Unit 1.
- If you plan to have students use the **Outline worksheet** and **Peer evaluation form**, or if you plan to use the **Assessment form** during students' presentations, be sure to make the appropriate number of copies before students begin their presentations.
- When students finish their presentations, have them complete the **Self-evaluation** on page 81 in their Student's Books.

Unit 2	Teacher's Manual page
Language summary	53
Outline worksheet	59
Peer evaluation form	64
Assessment form	65

3 *Dream vacation*

Overview

In this unit, students talk about different types of vacations and their travel preferences. They practice describing vacation destinations, activities, and accommodations. In preparation for their own presentations about a dream vacation, students look at brainstorming notes, complete a presentation outline, and listen to a model presentation about a dream vacation. They then practice using lead-in questions to generate interest in the topic and, finally, prepare and give their own presentations about a dream vacation.

Lesson	Activities
Topic focus	Discussing types of vacations; planning the perfect vacation
Language focus	Talking about vacation destinations; talking about activities and accommodations
Organization focus	Focusing on brainstorming ideas and creating an outline for a presentation about a dream vacation
Presentation focus	Focusing on the introduction, body, and conclusion of a presentation; listening to a model presentation about a dream vacation: *South Island Adventure*
Presentation skills focus	Asking lead-in questions; timing and intonation of lead-in questions
Present yourself!	Brainstorming ideas; creating an outline; giving a presentation about a dream vacation

Topic focus

1 Vacations
Page 32

> **Teaching tip** As this unit focuses on travel destinations around the world, it may be useful to have a world map in the classroom so you can point out some of the destinations to students.

Notes

Useful language

ecotour a trip to a natural environment that does not cause harm to nature

endangered animals or plants that might stop existing because there are only a few alive

habitat the natural surrounding in which plants or animals live

historic having importance in the past (see *Usage tip* below)

luxury great comfort provided by expensive things that are enjoyable but often not necessary

to observe to watch something or someone carefully

rain forest a large area of tropical forest where it rains at least 250 centimeters a year (for example, the Amazon rain forest)

safari a trip to watch, photograph, or hunt wild animals

species a set of animals or plants that have similar characteristics

wildlife wild animals and plants living in nature

Usage tip

historic / historical

Many learners confuse the words *historic* and *historical*. While *historic* describes something with importance in the past, for example, a historic building, *historical* describes something related to or based on history, for example, historical documents.

Warm-up

- Books closed. To introduce the topic, tell students to imagine that they have won a vacation to a destination of their choice. Ask students where they would go, what type of vacation they would take, and how they would spend their vacation. Elicit responses from a few students.

A

- Have students form pairs and tell them to open to page 32 in their Student's Books.
- Read the instructions aloud.
- Read the names of the vacations aloud, and have students repeat them. Explain any unfamiliar language.
- Give students about three minutes to discuss where they think the places are.
- Walk around the classroom, helping students as necessary.
- Ask for volunteers to share their guesses before you go over the answers with the class.

Possible answers		
1. Africa	3. Cambodia	5. Brazil
2. Hawaii	4. South America	6. Caribbean Sea

B

- Read the instructions aloud.
- Call on individual students to read the partial sentences aloud. Explain any unfamiliar language.
- Point out the example answer.
- Give students about three minutes to match the pictures to the descriptions.
- Walk around the classroom, helping students as necessary.
- Go over the answers with the whole class.

Answers

1. want to observe animals in their natural habitats
2. need to get away from it all and enjoy the sun and sand
3. like to visit world-famous attractions and learn about the past
4. want an exciting, active vacation
5. are concerned about the environment and want to help save endangered species
6. enjoy traveling in comfort and style

C

- Read the instructions aloud.
- To help students get started, read the model language aloud, completing it with your own ideas.
- Ask for a few volunteers to share their responses with the class.

② Travel preferences interview
Page 33

A

- Tell students that they will now have a chance to find out about their classmates' travel preferences.
- Read the instructions aloud.
- Call on individual students to read the interview questions aloud.
- Give students about two minutes to write one more interview question.
- Walk around the classroom, helping students as necessary.
- Have students form pairs.
- Give pairs about five minutes to complete their interviews. Remind students that they should take notes on their partners' answers because they will need the information when they do Exercise B.

B

- Combine pairs to form groups of four.
- Read the instructions aloud.
- Point out the model language to help students get started.
- Give groups about five minutes to share their information.
- Ask for a few volunteers to share information about their classmates' travel preferences.

③ My perfect vacation
Page 33

> **Notes**
>
> **Useful language**
> **accommodations** a place to stay while traveling
> **bed-and-breakfast** a small hotel that rents rooms and provides a morning meal
> **bungalow** a small house all on one level
> **cabin** a small, simple house
> **Oceania** a geographical region in the South Pacific Ocean that includes Australia, New Zealand, and a large number of smaller islands
> **youth hostel** a large house where young people can stay cheaply while traveling

A

- Read the instructions aloud.
- Call on individual students to read the categories and the options in the vacation planner aloud. Explain any unfamiliar language.
- Give students about two minutes to circle (or write) their choices.

B

- Read the instructions aloud.
- Point out the model language to help students get started.

- Ask for a few volunteers to share their responses with the class.
- Lead a brief class discussion about the most popular choices from the vacation planner. Ask students why they think those choices were the most popular.

Language focus

❶ Vacation destinations
Page 34

> **Teaching tip** Before you begin this lesson, you may want to prepare some photos of the places discussed (Borneo, Maui, and Rome) to bring to class. This will help generate more interest.

Notes

Useful language

delightful enjoyable; full of pleasure
exotic unusual and especially interesting
fabulous very good; wonderful
highlight the best, most exciting part
nightlife entertainment that happens especially in nightclubs in the evening
romantic relating to love
scenic having beautiful natural surroundings
situated located in a particular place

Culture tip

Borneo is the third largest island in the world and is divided between Indonesia, Malaysia, and Brunei. The Borneo rain forest is the only natural habitat for the endangered Bornean orangutan.
Maui is the second largest of the Hawaiian islands. The island welcomes more than two million tourists every year.
Rome is the capital city of Italy and is home to some of the world's most famous historic landmarks such as the Colosseum, the Roman Forum, and the Pantheon.

Warm-up

- Books closed. If you have photos (see *Teaching tip* above), show them to the class. If not, write the names of the three places on the board. Ask students what they know about these places (see *Notes* above). Tell students they are going to learn more about these popular vacation destinations.

A

- Tell students to open to page 34 in their Student's Books.
- Have students look at the pictures.
- Ask if anyone has been to any of the three places, and if so, to describe the trip and their impressions.
- Read the instructions aloud.

- Elicit a few responses to the questions. Encourage students to make guesses about what people can see or do at each place.

Possible answers

1. **Borneo:** see wild animals, hike through the jungle
2. **Maui:** enjoy nature, see a volcano
3. **Rome:** sightsee, learn about history

B   Track 11

- Read the instructions aloud.
- Read the answer choices in the chart aloud, and have students repeat them. Explain any unfamiliar language.
- Play the audio program once or twice as needed.
- Have students compare answers in pairs before you go over the answers with the whole class.

Answers

1. **Borneo:** Southeast, exotic, wildlife
2. **Maui:** northwest, beautiful, accommodations
3. **Rome:** middle, romantic, restaurants

C

- Tell students that they are now going to play a guessing game about popular vacation destinations.
- Have students form pairs.
- Read the instructions aloud.
- Read the language in the box aloud, and have students repeat it. If necessary, encourage students to use this language when they do the activity.
- Point out the model language to help students get started.

> **Teaching tip** You may want to do a few examples with the whole class before students play the game in pairs. Describe places, or ask for a few students to describe places, while the class tries to guess.

- Give students about five minutes to play the game.
- Walk around the classroom, helping students as necessary.

❷ Activities and accommodations
Page 35

Notes

Useful language

architecture the style of a building
five-star the best rating for hotels and restaurants
journey a trip, especially over a long period or great distance
jungle a forest in one of the hot areas of the earth
paradise a beautiful, perfect place

A 💿 Track 12

- Read the instructions aloud.
- Give students about one minute to read the information in the chart. Explain any unfamiliar language.
- Play the audio program once or twice as needed.
- Check answers by calling on individual students to say the activities and accommodations for each vacation.

Answers

1. **Borneo Jungle Ecotour**
   hike through the jungle, go on a night safari; tents
2. **Maui Island Paradise**
   spend time shopping, watch the sunset; five-star resort
3. **Journey Through Historic Rome**
   learn about art and architecture, visit the countryside; bed-and-breakfast

B

- Have students form pairs.
- Read the instructions aloud.
- To help students get started, read the model language aloud, completing it with your own ideas.
- Give pairs about five minutes to discuss the activities and accommodations. Remind them to add their own ideas.
- Walk around the classroom, helping students as necessary.
- Ask for a few volunteers to share their responses with the class.

③ Let's go!
Page 35

Notes

Usage tip

opportunity / chance
These words have the same meaning in this context, but *opportunity* is more formal than *chance*.

A

- Read the instructions aloud.

Teaching tip You may want to tell students that, if they like, they can choose a destination other than the one they chose in Exercise C on page 34.

- Give students about two minutes to write their information.
- Walk around the classroom, helping students as necessary.

B

- Have students form groups of three or four.
- Read the instructions aloud.

- Read the language in the box aloud, and have students repeat it. If necessary, encourage students to use this language when they do the activity.
- Point out the model language at the bottom of the page to help students get started.
- Give groups about five minutes to share their information.
- Ask for a few volunteers to tell the class about some of the activities and accommodations they'd like to try.

Organization focus

① Sam's dream vacation
Page 36

Notes

Useful language

dolphin a sea mammal that looks like a large fish and has a pointed mouth

whale watching going out to sea in a boat to see whales

Culture note

Maori

The *Maori*, the original people of New Zealand, came from Polynesia and the Pacific islands to the north and east of New Zealand.

A

- Have students form pairs.
- Tell students to open to page 36 in their Student's Books, but have them cover Exercises B and C and page 37. Tell them to look only at the picture while you read the instructions and questions aloud.
- Give pairs about one minute to discuss the picture.
- Ask for a few volunteers to share their responses with the class.

Possible answers

It's beautiful / natural / clean / scenic.
People can go hiking / go swimming / spend time outdoors.

- Tell students they are going to find out more information about Sam's dream vacation in this lesson and in the next lesson of the unit.

B

- Have students uncover their books.
- Read the instructions aloud.
- Have students look at the brainstorming map and at the outline on page 37.
- Give students about two minutes to check the eight topics included in the outline.
- Go over the answers with the whole class.

c

> **Teaching tip** You may want to have students do this exercise in pairs, so they can help each other and share ideas.

■ Read the instructions aloud.

■ Give students time to read the notes. Explain any unfamiliar language.

■ Give students about three minutes to complete the outline.

■ Walk around the classroom, helping students as necessary.

■ If students have been working individually, have them compare their answers in pairs.

❷ Sam's outline 💿 Track 13
Page 37

> **Notes**
>
> **Useful language**
>
> **canoe** a small, light, narrow boat pointed at both ends and moved by a person with a paddle
>
> **cave** a large hole in the side of a hill or mountain, or underground
>
> **fascinating** very interesting
>
> **to paddle** to move a boat through water by using a stick with a wide flat end
>
> **trek** a long walk, usually in the country; a hike
>
> **Culture tip**
>
> **Kiwi**
>
> The *kiwi* is a small, flightless, nocturnal bird and is the national symbol of New Zealand. There are five species of kiwi, all of which are endangered. In North American English, the word *kiwi* is often used for both the bird and the kiwifruit. However, New Zealanders use the word *kiwi* uniquely for the bird, and *kiwifruit* for the fruit. *Kiwi* can also be used to describe a person from New Zealand.

■ Read the instructions aloud.

■ Play the audio program and have students follow along with the outline.

■ Check answers by reading through the outline aloud and calling on individual students to say the missing information.

Presentation focus

❶ Introduction
Pages 38 and 39

> **Teaching tip** Before doing this lesson, you may want to encourage students to review the vocabulary and language presented in Unit 3. Hand out a copy of the Unit 3 **Language summary** (Teacher's Manual page 54) to each student in the class. Alternatively, refer students to the appropriate sections in their Student's Books if they need help completing the tasks.

> **Teaching tip** At this point, or at some point in this lesson, you may want to show students a map of New Zealand and locate the places mentioned in the presentation.

■ Tell students they are now going to focus on each section of Sam's presentation separately.

■ Read the instructions aloud.

■ Read the bullet points and the model language aloud. If necessary, remind students that the missing words in the presentation can all be found on pages 34 to 37.

■ Give students about two minutes to read and complete the introduction.

■ Walk around the classroom, helping students as necessary.

❷ Body
Pages 38 and 39

> **Notes**
>
> **Useful language**
>
> **cozy** comfortable, pleasant, and inviting
>
> **luxurious** very comfortable and usually expensive; usually not necessary
>
> **picturesque** attractive in appearance
>
> **stunning** extremely beautiful

- Read the instructions aloud.
- Call on a student to read the bullet points aloud.
- Give students about three minutes to read and complete the body.
- Walk around the classroom, helping students as necessary.

③ Conclusion
Pages 38 and 39

> **Notes**
>
> **Useful language**
> **breathtaking** extremely beautiful

- Read the instructions aloud.
- Call on a student to read the bullet points and the model language aloud.
- Give students about two minutes to read and complete the conclusion.
- Walk around the classroom, helping students as necessary.

④ Sam's presentation 💿 Track 13
Pages 38 and 39

- Read the instructions aloud.
- Play the audio program and have students check their answers.
- Ask for volunteers to read sections of the presentation aloud, inserting the missing words.
- Write the correct answers on the board for students' reference.

> **Answers**
>
> **Introduction:** nature, exciting
> **Body:** most, known, offers, can, able, chance, opportunity, able, hotel
> **Conclusion:** activities, scenery

> **Teaching tip** You may want to finish by having students talk about their own travel experiences and preferences. Write questions on the board, and have students discuss them in pairs or small groups. For example:
> *Do you prefer nature or the city? Why?*
> *Have you ever been on a trek? Where? When? Would you like to? Why? Why not?*
> *What part of Sam's vacation do you think you would enjoy the most?*

Presentation skills focus

① Lead-in questions
Page 40

> **Notes**
>
> **Useful language**
> **brochure** a small magazine or pamphlet containing pictures and information about a product or a company
> **curiosity** a desire to know and learn about something
> **to escape** to become free from
> **to be fed up** to be annoyed to the point where you feel a situation shouldn't continue
> **gourmet meal** a high-quality meal, often with unusual or special ingredients

Warm-up

- Books closed. Ask students to think back to the introduction of Sam's presentation. Try to elicit the two questions Sam used to start his presentation, and write them on the board. (*Are you looking for some excitement? Do you want to experience exotic cultures?*) If necessary, have students open to page 39 in their Student's Books to look again at the presentation and find the two questions.
- Ask students to think of examples of similar questions they may have read or heard, for example, in TV commercials, or in magazine or newspaper ads. Write them on the board as students say them. Finally, tell students that these are called *lead-in questions*, and that in a presentation, they can be a useful way to generate interest in the topic.

▼

- Tell students to open to page 40 in their Student's Books.
- Read the information at the top of the page aloud.
- Read the instructions aloud.
- Call on individual students to read the lead-in questions aloud.
- Have students work alone or in pairs to match the questions to the pictures.
- Walk around the classroom, helping students as necessary.
- Go over the answers with the whole class.

- Ask for a volunteer to read the presentation tip aloud.

> **Teaching tip** You may want to model the presentation tip by reading two of the questions on page 40 aloud and then calling on individual students to do the same with those or other questions.

➋ Your turn
Page 41

A

- Read the instructions aloud.
- Call on individual students to read the language from the box aloud.
- Give students about five minutes to write their lead-in questions.
- Walk around the classroom, helping students as necessary.

Possible answers

1. Are you looking for an empty beach?
2. Do you love active vacations?
3. Are you tired of rundown hotels?
4. Do you want to spend time with your family?
5. Are you fed up with working too much?
6. Do you need a relaxing vacation?

B

- Have students form pairs.
- Read the instructions aloud.
- Point out the model language to help students get started.
- Give pairs about five minutes to ask their questions. Remind them not to ask the questions in order.
- To finish, continue the activity with the whole class. Call on individual students to ask one of their questions, and have the rest of the class guess the picture.

C

- Read the instructions aloud.
- Ask for volunteers to read the example introductions aloud. Explain any unfamiliar language.
- Give students about five minutes to write their questions.

- Walk around the classroom, helping students as necessary.

D

- Have students form pairs.
- Read the instructions aloud.
- Give students about two minutes to practice reading the introductions in Exercise C individually. Then have them stand and take turns reading the introductions aloud. Remind them to follow the presentation tip on page 40. Encourage them to also use the presentation skills they learned in earlier units (for example, making eye contact with the audience).
- Walk around the classroom, helping students as necessary.
- When students finish, tell them that they are now ready to begin planning their own presentations about a dream vacation.

Present yourself!

➊ Brainstorming
Page 42

- Read the assignment in the box at the top of the page aloud.
- Read the instructions aloud.
- Give students time to choose a destination. If they need help doing this, refer them to pages 32 and 33 in their Student's Books for ideas.
- Have students complete the brainstorming map. Remind them not to write complete sentences. They should brainstorm as much information as possible about their destinations and make brief notes.
- Walk around the classroom, helping students as necessary.
- If students need help, refer them to the example brainstorming map on page 36 (Exercise B) in their Student's Books. Alternatively, have students watch while you draw a brainstorming map with notes about a favorite vacation destination of yours on the board. Then review the brainstorming map with the students.

➋ Organizing
Page 43

> **Teaching tip** Depending on your available class time, you may want to have students start this activity in class and finish it as homework.

- Read the instructions aloud.
- Have students read the topics in the outline.
- Give students time to think of a presentation title and complete the outline.
- Walk around the classroom, helping students as necessary.

> **Teaching tip** If students need more help organizing their outlines, you may want to collect the outlines and give written feedback on them to the students.

- Have students make their final notes on note cards. Remind them that they should speak from abbreviated notes written on note cards, and should not read out their presentations word for word.
- Remind students to practice their presentations.

> **Teaching tip** If time allows, you may want to have students form pairs or groups and take turns practicing their presentations in class. Suggest that students ask a classmate to time the length of their presentations, and encourage them to make suggestions to help improve their classmates' presentations.

❸ Presenting
Page 43

> **Teaching tip** Depending on your class size, you will need to determine the best format (group or whole class) and time limit for students' presentations.

- Read the instructions aloud.
- Explain the format and time limit for students' presentations (see *Teaching tip* on the left). Make sure students understand that they will be expected to use the language and presentation skills they learned in Unit 3, as well as any appropriate language and skills they have learned in the course so far.
- If you plan to have students use the **Outline worksheet** and **Peer evaluation form**, or if you plan to use the **Assessment form** during students' presentations, be sure to make the appropriate number of copies before students begin their presentations.
- When students finish their presentations, have them complete the **Self-evaluation** on page 82 in their Student's Books.

Unit 3	Teacher's Manual page
Language summary	54
Outline worksheet	60
Peer evaluation form	64
Assessment form	65

4 *How the world works*

Overview

In this unit, students talk about processes. They practice introducing a process presentation and explaining the stages of a process. In preparation for their own process presentations, students look at brainstorming notes, complete a presentation outline, and listen to a model process presentation. They then practice inviting audience questions and, finally, research a process and prepare and give their own process presentations.

Lesson	Activities
Topic focus	Taking a trivia quiz; talking about process topics
Language focus	Introducing a process presentation; explaining a process
Organization focus	Focusing on brainstorming ideas and creating an outline for a process presentation
Presentation focus	Focusing on the introduction, body, and conclusion of a presentation; listening to a model process presentation: *Coffee Manufacturing: From Bean to Cup*
Presentation skills focus	Inviting audience questions; answering audience questions
Present yourself!	Researching a process; creating an outline; giving a presentation about the process

Topic focus

1 Trivia quiz
Page 44

Notes

Useful language

consumer product an item for sale in a store

culture shock a feeling of confusion when you are in a different culture

earthquake a sudden shaking movement in the ground

to elect to choose a person for a particular job by voting

geologist a scientist who studies rocks and the physical makeup of the earth

meteorologist a scientist who studies weather and climate

pixel the smallest unit of an image on a TV or computer screen

rainbow an arch of many colors that sometimes appears in the sky for a short time after rain

seismologist a scientist who studies earthquakes

surface the outer or top layer of something

trivia unimportant or little-known facts or details

Warm-up

■ Books closed. Ask students if they watch quiz shows on TV. Find out which quiz shows they like to watch, and what kind of topics are usually included on quiz shows. Guide them to the idea that the kind of knowledge that is often on quiz shows is not really important to know, but is often fun and interesting.

■ Explain or elicit the meaning of *trivia* (see *Notes* above). Tell students that they now will have the chance to test their trivia knowledge about how the world works.

A

■ Tell students to open to page 44 in their Student's Books.

■ Read the instructions aloud.

- Tell students to look over the quiz first and to circle any words they don't know. Encourage them to ask their classmates to explain any unfamiliar language. Then go over any language students still don't understand.
- Give students about five minutes to take the quiz. Encourage them to make guesses when they don't know an answer.
- Walk around the classroom, helping students as necessary.
- Have students compare answers in pairs. Then tell them to check their answers using the answer key at the bottom of the quiz.
- Ask for a few volunteers to share any questions they thought were especially challenging, quiz answers that surprised them, and information they already knew and how they knew it.

B

- Have students stay in their pairs from Exercise A.
- Read the instructions aloud.
- Give students about three minutes to write their quiz questions. Make sure students understand that they must know the correct answers to their questions.
- Walk around the classroom, helping students as necessary.
- Give students about five minutes to ask one another their quiz questions.
- To finish, have the whole class play a trivia quiz game. Divide the class into two teams. Have volunteers from each team take turns asking their quiz questions, and have the other team answer. Keep score on the board.

② Process topics
Page 45

Notes

Useful language

ceremony a set of traditional or religious acts performed at a special occasion

conference a large, formal meeting at which there are groups of talks on a particular subject

cycle a series of stages, events, or steps that repeat themselves

to erupt to burst out suddenly or explode

formation the process by which something is formed or made

hybrid car a car that uses a combination of fuels to run (*hybrid* = mixed or blended)

process a series of actions to make something or achieve a particular result

tsunami a giant ocean wave; also called a tidal wave

volcano a mountain made from burned rock that may explode and throw out hot liquid rock (lava)

A

- Read the instructions aloud.
- Call on individual students to read the topics aloud. Explain any unfamiliar language.
- Give students a few minutes to read the conference schedule. Encourage them to ask their classmates to explain any unfamiliar language. Then go over any language students still don't understand.
- Point out the example answer.
- Give students about five minutes to match the presentations to the topics. Make sure students understand that they will need to use each topic more than once and that some presentations may match more than one topic.
- Walk around the classroom, helping students as necessary.
- Have students compare answers in pairs. Then ask for volunteers to share their answers with the class.

Answers

c: How Are Rainbows Formed?

a, d: Understanding the Internet

b: The Sleep Cycle

e: The Art of the Japanese Tea Ceremony

c: Tsunami Formation

a, d: How Text Messaging Works

a, d: How Hybrid Cars Work

a: Herbal Tea: A Growing Business

b: How Do People Hear?

e: The U.S. Election Process

a: The Secrets of Ice-Cream Making

c: Why Do Volcanoes Erupt?

B

- Combine pairs to form groups of four.
- Read the instructions aloud.
- Point out the written example.
- Give groups about five minutes to choose their topics and write their presentation titles.
- Walk around the classroom, helping students as necessary.

C

- Read the instructions aloud.
- Call on two students to read the model language aloud. Ask the class if anyone can finish the explanation of how thunder happens. (. . . *when warm air expands, as a result of electricity from lightning, and creates a sound.*)
- Ask for a volunteer from each group to share the group's presentation titles.
- As each title is read out, encourage students to share what they know about the topic.

Language focus

❶ Introducing a process presentation
Page 46

Notes

Useful language

to cure to solve a health problem

damage the harm done to an area, a building, or an object

disorder an illness of the mind or body

to influence to affect

to occur to happen

pollution dirt or chemicals that make air or water unclean and harmful to people, animals, and plants

to rescue to save

tide the rising and falling of the sea that happens twice every day

A ⊙ Track 14

- Have students look at the pictures while you read the instructions aloud.
- Ask for volunteers to read the presentation titles below the pictures aloud. Explain any unfamiliar language.
- Play the audio program once or twice as needed.
- Have students compare answers in pairs before you go over the answers with the whole class.

Answers

1. **Kazu:** The Sleep Cycle
2. **Tami:** Tsunami Formation

B ⊙ Track 14

- Read the instructions aloud.
- Give students about one minute to read the information. Explain any unfamiliar language.
- Play the audio program once or twice as needed.
- Ask for volunteers to share their answers with the class.

Answers

1. **Kazu:**
   what the stages of sleep are called
   when dreams are created
   how the brain is affected
2. **Tami:**
   which places are affected
   what kinds of damage are caused
   how the waves are formed

C

- Tell students that they are now going to play the roles of the two speakers from Exercises A and B: Kazu and Tami.
- Have students form pairs.
- Read the instructions aloud.

- Read the language in the box aloud, and have students repeat it. If necessary, encourage students to use this language when they do the activity.
- Point out the model language to help students get started.
- Give pairs about three minutes to introduce the presentations. Tell students they can use the information in Exercise B to help them.
- Walk around the classroom, helping students as necessary.
- Call on individual students to describe each presentation to the class.

❷ How does it happen?
Page 47

Notes

Useful language

brain waves the activity of the brain that can only be monitored on special medical equipment

drowsiness a feeling of sleepiness

heart rate the number of times that the heart beats in a given time

to investigate to look for and find out the facts about something

REM rapid eye movement

reporter a person who writes articles for newspapers or magazines

shore the coast or edge of land next to a body of water

Grammar tip

The passive voice

This lesson provides a good opportunity to teach (or review) the passive voice. Explain to students that the passive voice is often used when describing a process. It is formed by using the present or past of the verb *be* plus the past participle, for example, *are slowed*, *is lowered*, or *was destroyed*. Have students try to find all the examples of the passive voice in the *Language focus* lesson.

Warm-up

- Books closed. Write the two presentation titles from Exercise A on page 46 on the board (*The Sleep Cycle*, *Tsunami Formation*). Tell students that after they introduce the topic of a process presentation, they need to explain how the process happens.
- Have students form pairs or small groups so they can work together to come up with a brief explanation for how the two processes on the board happen. Encourage students to make guesses if they don't know the information.
- Elicit explanations from the pairs (or groups).

A ⊙ Track 15

- Tell students to open to page 47 in their Student's Books.

- Read the instructions aloud.
- Point out to students that the first one has been matched for them.
- Ask for volunteers to read the information under *The stages* and *What happens* aloud. Explain any unfamiliar language.
- Give students about three minutes to match the stages to what happens.
- Play the audio program once or twice as needed and have students check their guesses. Then go over the answers with the whole class.

Answers

1. a: The eyes first close.
   b: The heart rate is lowered.
   c: The brain waves are slowed.
   d: Dreaming begins.
2. a: The ocean floor moves suddenly.
   b: The water level rises slightly.
   c: The waves gain speed and strength.
   d: Houses and buildings are destroyed.

B

- Have students form pairs.
- Read the instructions aloud.
- Read the language in the box aloud, and have students repeat it. If necessary, encourage them to use this language when they do the activity.
- Make sure students understand the difference between *named* and *unnamed* stages; use the example of numbers 1 and 2 in Exercise A. The stages in number 1 are named (drowsiness, light sleep, etc.), and the stages in number 2 are unnamed.
- Give pairs about five minutes to explain the processes in Exercise A. Encourage them to practice their explanations a few times, and then to try saying them without looking at the language in the box.
- Walk around the classroom, helping students as necessary.
- Play track 15 of the audio program one more time, so that students can hear the original explanations again.

C

- Have students change partners.
- Read the instructions aloud.
- Model the task by reading the model language aloud and calling on a student to complete it. Point out that the stages in this process are not named; therefore, they begin with the phrase, *In the (first) stage, . . .*
- Give pairs about five minutes to explain the process.
- Walk around the classroom, helping students as necessary.
- Ask for volunteers to explain the process to the class.

> **Teaching tip** For higher-level classes, have students close their books and try explaining the process.

Organization focus

1 Nicole's process presentation
Page 48

Notes

Useful language

to brew to make a drink by pouring water through dry, ground ingredients

to grind to crush something into very small pieces or into a powder

to harvest to pick or gather a crop that is ripe

to process (food) to prepare or treat food so that it can be sold or consumed

raw uncooked

to roast to cook by dry heat in an oven

sack a large bag, usually made of cloth or paper

to sort to separate into different types

A

- Tell students to open to page 48 in their Student's Books, but have them cover Exercises B and C and page 49. Tell them to look only at the picture while you read the instructions and the questions aloud.
- Elicit a few responses to the questions.

Possible answers

It's a coffee plantation (farm) in Brazil / Costa Rica / Hawaii.

The person is picking coffee beans.

- Tell students they are going to find out more information about the coffee-manufacturing process in this lesson and in the next lesson of the unit.

B

- Have students uncover their books.
- Read the instructions aloud.
- Have students look at the brainstorming notes and at the outline on page 49.
- Give students about two minutes to check the eight topics included in the outline.
- Go over the answers with the whole class.

Answers

A preview of the presentation

Second stage: processing

Recommendations for further research

A review of all the stages of the process

First stage: growing and harvesting

An interesting fact about the process

Third stage: roasting

Final stage: grinding and brewing

c

> **Teaching tip** You may want to have students do this exercise in pairs, so they can help each other and share ideas.

- Read the instructions aloud.
- Give students time to read the notes. Explain any unfamiliar language.
- Give students about three minutes to complete the outline.
- Walk around the classroom, helping students as necessary.
- If students have been working individually, have them compare their answers in pairs.

② Nicole's outline ● Track 16
Page 49

> **Notes**
>
> **Useful language**
> **to trade** to buy and sell or to swap

- Read the instructions aloud.
- Play the audio program and have students follow along with the outline.
- Check answers by reading through the outline aloud and calling on individual students to say the missing information.

> **Answers**
>
> I.   B. 2. go over how raw beans are processed
> II. A. 3. coffee cherries are picked by hand or machine
> II. B. 3. beans are dried, sorted, put into sacks for shipping
> II. C. 1. beans are heated to 240°C in roasting machine
> II. D. 1. whole beans are crushed, mixed with hot water
> III. A. 4. grinding and brewing

Presentation focus

① Introduction
Pages 50 and 51

> **Teaching tip** Before doing this lesson, you may want to encourage students to review the vocabulary and language presented in Unit 4. Hand out a copy of the Unit 4 **Language summary** (Teacher's Manual page 55) to each student in the class. Alternatively, refer students to the appropriate sections in their Student's Books if they need help completing the tasks.

- Tell students they are now going to focus on each section of Nicole's presentation separately.
- Read the instructions aloud.
- Read the bullet points and the model language aloud. If necessary, remind students that the missing words in the presentation can all be found on pages 46 to 49.
- Give students about two minutes to read and complete the introduction.
- Walk around the classroom, helping students as necessary.

② Body
Pages 50 and 51

> **Notes**
>
> **Useful language**
> **Celsius** the metric system of measuring temperature; also called centigrade

- Read the instructions aloud.
- Ask for a volunteer to read the bullet points aloud.
- Give students about three minutes to read and complete the body.
- Walk around the classroom, helping students as necessary.

③ Conclusion
Pages 50 and 51

- Read the instructions aloud.
- Ask for a volunteer to read the bullet points and the model language aloud.
- Give students about two minutes to read and complete the conclusion.
- Walk around the classroom, helping students as necessary.

④ Nicole's presentation ● Track 16
Pages 50 and 51

- Read the instructions aloud.
- Have students compare answers in pairs.
- Play the audio program and have students check their answers.
- Call on individual students to write the correct answers on the board.

> **Answers**
>
> **Introduction:** product, In, over
> **Body:** During, point, when, stage, third, final
> **Conclusion:** harvesting, grinding

Presentation skills focus

1 Inviting audience questions
Page 52

Notes

Useful language
to interrupt to stop someone from speaking

Warm-up

- Books closed. Ask students to think back to the introduction of Nicole's presentation. Ask, *What does Nicole say she will do when she finishes the presentation?* (Take questions from the audience.) If necessary, have students open to page 51 in their Student's Books and look again at the presentation.

- Tell students that in a process presentation, it is helpful to give the audience some time to ask questions if:
  - they didn't understand a part of the presentation and they want more details;
  - they want to confirm their notes;
  - they want more information about a point.

- Explain that in this lesson, students are going to practice inviting audience questions.

▼

- Tell students to open to page 52 in their Student's Books.
- Read the information at the top of the page aloud.
- Read the instructions aloud.
- Call on individual students to read the sentences for inviting audience questions aloud. Explain any unfamiliar language.
- Point out the example answer.
- Give students about three minutes to write their answers.
- Walk around the classroom, helping students as necessary.
- Read the sentences aloud, and ask for volunteers to say whether they are used for inviting questions during or after the presentation.

Answers

D = during, A = after
A: I'll be happy to take your questions when I'm finished.
D: Feel free to interrupt me if you have questions.
D: If you have questions, please ask them at any time.
A: I'll take questions after the presentation.
A: Please hold your questions until the end.
D: Please stop me at any time if you have questions.

- Ask for a volunteer to read the presentation tip aloud.

2 Your turn
Page 53

A

- Read the instructions aloud.
- Give students time to read the beginnings of the introductions. Explain any unfamiliar language.
- Give students about five minutes to complete the introductions.
- Walk around the classroom, helping students as necessary.

B

- Have students form pairs.
- Read the instructions aloud.
- Give pairs about five minutes to share their introductions. Remind students to follow the presentation tip on page 52. Encourage them to also use the presentation skills they learned in earlier units (for example, making eye contact with the audience).
- Walk around the classroom, helping students as necessary.
- Call on a few students to share their introductions with the class.

C

- Have students change partners.
- Read the instructions aloud.
- Call on individual students to read the process topics aloud. Explain any unfamiliar language.
- Point out the model language to help students get started.
- Give pairs about five minutes to introduce the topic and invite audience questions. Remind students to follow the presentation tip on page 52. Encourage them to also use the presentation skills they learned in earlier units (for example, making eye contact with the audience).
- Ask for volunteers to present one of their introductions to the class.
- When students finish, tell them that they are now ready to begin planning their own process presentations.

Present yourself!

❶ Brainstorming
Page 54

> **Teaching tip** As this presentation requires students to do research on a process, plan to begin the brainstorming process in class. Then allot the remaining class time for students' research, and assign the rest of the research as homework.

- Read the assignment in the box at the top of the page aloud.
- Read the instructions aloud.
- Give students time to choose a process. If they need help doing this, refer them to pages 44 and 45 for ideas.
- Have students brainstorm information and complete their research. Remind students not to write complete sentences. They should brainstorm and research as much information as possible about the process and make brief notes.
- Walk around the classroom, helping students as necessary.
- If students need help, refer them to the example brainstorming notes on page 48 (Exercise B) in their Student's Books. Alternatively, have the class choose an example process. Then elicit some possible details for each brainstorming topic and write them on the board.

❷ Organizing
Page 55

> **Teaching tip** Depending on your available class time, you may want to have students start this activity in class and finish it as homework.

- Read the instructions aloud.
- Have students read the topics in the outline.
- Give students time to think of a presentation title and complete the outline.
- Walk around the classroom, helping students as necessary.

> **Teaching tip** If students need more help organizing their outlines, you may want to collect the outlines and give written feedback on them to the students.

- Have students make their final notes on note cards. Remind them that they should speak from abbreviated notes written on note cards, and should not read out their presentations word for word.
- Remind students to practice their presentations.

> **Teaching tip** If time allows, you may want to have students form pairs or groups and take turns practicing their presentations in class. Suggest that students ask a classmate to time the length of their presentations, and encourage them to make suggestions to help improve their classmates' presentations.

❸ Presenting
Page 55

> **Teaching tip** Depending on your class size, you will need to determine the best format (group or whole class) and time limit for students' presentations.

- Read the instructions aloud.
- Explain the format and time limit for students' presentations (see *Teaching tip* above). Make sure students understand that they will be expected to use the language and presentation skills they learned in Unit 4, as well as any appropriate language and skills they have learned in the course so far.
- If you plan to have students use the **Outline worksheet** and **Peer evaluation form**, or if you plan to use the **Assessment form** during students' presentations, be sure to make the appropriate number of copies before students begin their presentations.
- When students finish their presentations, have them complete the **Self-evaluation** on page 83 in their Student's Books.

Unit 4	Teacher's Manual page
Language summary	55
Outline worksheet	61
Peer evaluation form	64
Assessment form	65

5 *In my opinion*

Overview

In this unit, students identify and discuss issues they feel strongly about. They practice expressing an opposing opinion and using supporting information. In preparation for their own persuasive presentations, students look at brainstorming notes, complete a presentation outline, and listen to a model persuasive presentation. They then practice emphasizing an opposing opinion and, finally, prepare and give their own persuasive presentations about an issue.

Lesson	Activities
Topic focus	Discussing issues; completing an opinions survey
Language focus	Relating an issue and expressing an opposing opinion; supporting opinions
Organization focus	Focusing on brainstorming ideas and creating an outline for a persuasive presentation
Presentation focus	Focusing on the introduction, body, and conclusion of a presentation; listening to a model persuasive presentation: *People Should Stop Eating Meat*
Presentation skills focus	Emphasizing an opposing opinion; using body language to emphasize an opinion
Present yourself!	Brainstorming ideas; creating an outline; giving a presentation about an important issue

Topic focus

❶ Issues
Page 56

Notes

Useful language

global warming a gradual increase in the earth's temperature caused by gases such as carbon dioxide

issue a subject or problem that people are thinking about

lifestyle a way of living that includes what people own, their interests, and their activities

media newspapers, the Internet, magazines, television, and radio, considered as a group

medical of or relating to medicine

politics the activities of the government or those who work for the government

to raise (children) to care for and teach children until they reach adulthood

to recycle to process (paper, plastic, glass, etc.) for a new use

society people considered as a group

tax money paid to the government, usually a percentage of a person's income or of the price of purchased goods

tuition the money paid for being taught, especially at a university

uniform a special set of clothes worn by people belonging to the same organization

violence extremely forceful actions intended to hurt people

volunteer working without pay

Culture tip

Expressing disagreement

Some students, particularly those from Asian cultures, may feel uncomfortable expressing disagreement with their classmates' (or your) opinions. Before you begin this unit, you may want to discuss this issue with the class. Tell students that in many cultures, it is common for people to discuss their opinions openly, and to agree and disagree about social issues; it is not impolite or disrespectful.

Grammar tip

marriage / to marry

Note the various forms that learners often confuse: marriage (n.); get married (to someone); be married (to someone); to marry (someone)

Warm-up

- Books closed. Elicit some topics about which people often have differing opinions (for example, *art*, *the environment*, *fashion*, *music*, *politics*) and write the topics on the board. Then write the phrase *I believe . . .* on the board.
- Have students take out a piece of paper, and give them about two minutes to write as many opinions as they can about the topics on the board, using the phrase *I believe . . .* You may want to give them an example, such as, *I believe global warming is one of the most important issues today*.
- Have students form pairs and share their opinions. Encourage them to say whether they agree or disagree with their partners' opinions.
- Ask for a few volunteers to share their opinions with the class. Tell students that in this unit they will discuss their opinions and beliefs about different issues and try to persuade their classmates to agree with them.

A

- Tell students to open to page 56 in their Student's Books.
- Have students look at the pictures while you read the instructions aloud. Elicit the meaning of *issue* (see *Notes* on page 37).
- Ask for volunteers to read the banners and signs aloud. Explain (or have students explain to their classmates) any unfamiliar language.
- Have students discuss their ideas in pairs.
- Ask for volunteers to share their ideas with the class.

B

- Read the instructions aloud.
- Read the *Issues* in the box aloud, and have students repeat them. Explain any unfamiliar language.
- Give students time to read the categories in the chart. Explain any unfamiliar language.
- Point out the written example in the chart.
- Give students about five minutes to complete the chart.
- Walk around the classroom, helping students as necessary.
- Go over the answers with the whole class.
- Give students about two minutes to think of one more issue for each category.
- Ask for a few volunteers to share their ideas with the class.

Answers

Education: school uniforms, university tuition
The environment: global warming, recycling
Human relationships: marriage, raising children
Lifestyle and health: fast food, medical research
Media and technology: Internet use, violence on TV
Society and politics: taxes, volunteer work

Possible additional answers

Education: class sizes in schools
The environment: pollution
Human relationships: spending time with family
Lifestyle and health: health care systems
Media and technology: computer games
Society and politics: caring for elderly people

C

- Have students form pairs.
- Read the instructions aloud.
- Point out the model language to help students get started.
- Give students about two minutes to discuss their responses. Encourage students to give reasons for their opinions.
- Ask for a few volunteers to share their responses with the class. Encourage students to share their specific opinions and to give reasons for them.

❷ Opinions survey
Page 57

Notes

Useful language

advertising messages delivered to the public, usually in magazines or on TV, intended to make people want to buy a product

to aim (at) to direct at

banned not allowed; against the law

engine the machinery of a car that uses fuel to make the car move

to harm to hurt

wealthy having a lot of money

A

- Read the instructions aloud.
- Call on students to read the sentences in the left column of the survey aloud. Explain any unfamiliar language.
- Tell students that they should only check *not sure* if their opinion is really in the middle between *agree* and *disagree*. Alternatively, you could have students put two checks (✓✓) in the *agree* or *disagree* column if they have a strong opinion about an issue, and just one check (✓) if they basically agree or disagree.

- Give students about five minutes to complete the survey.
- Walk around the classroom, helping students as necessary.

B

- Have students form groups of three or four.
- Read the instructions aloud.
- Point out the model language to help students get started.
- Give students about 10 minutes to share their opinions. Remind them to explain the reasons for their choices.
- Walk around the classroom, helping students as necessary.
- Call on a few students to share some of their opinions and the reasons with the class.

❸ My opinions
Page 57

A

- Read the instructions aloud.
- Point out the written example in the chart.
- Give students about two minutes to complete the chart individually. Tell them that they can use issues from the opinions survey that they feel strongly about, or they can think of their own issues.
- Walk around the classroom, helping students as necessary.

B

- Have students form pairs.
- Read the instructions aloud.
- Point out the model language to help students get started.
- Give pairs about five minutes to share their information. Remind students to say whether they agree or disagree.
- Walk around the classroom, helping students as necessary.
- Ask for a few volunteers to share their opinions with the class.

Language focus

❶ Expressing opinions
Page 58

> **Notes**
>
> Useful language
> **opposing** disagreeing
> **rewarding** satisfying or beneficial

A

- Have students form pairs.

- Read the instructions aloud. Tell students that the issues can be found in the box on page 56.
- Give pairs about two minutes to compare their ideas.
- Walk around the classroom, helping students as necessary.
- Go over the answers with the whole class.

> **Answers**
>
> 1. school uniforms   2. Internet use   3. volunteer work

B 💿 Track 17

- Read the instructions aloud. Make sure students understand that they should check the picture that best illustrates the person's opinion.
- Encourage students to listen for key words that will help them choose the correct pictures.
- Play the audio program once or twice as needed.
- Have students compare answers in pairs before you go over the answers with the whole class.

> **Answers**
>
> 1. the student wearing a uniform
> 2. the child with her parent
> 3. the student planting a tree

- To finish, ask students to tell you what each person's opinion is. Have them complete the sentence, *Alex / Elena / Lisa thinks . . .*

C 💿 Track 17

- Read the instructions aloud.
- Call on individual students to read the reasons aloud. Explain any unfamiliar language.
- Play the audio program once or twice as needed.
- Have students compare answers in pairs before you go over the answers with the whole class.

> **Answers**
>
> 1. **Alex:**   2. **Elena:**
>   It saves money.   It's not controlled.
>   It improves schoolwork.   It can be dangerous.
> 3. **Lisa:**
>   It's educational.
>   It's rewarding.

D

- Have students form groups of three or four.
- Read the instructions aloud.
- Read the language in the box aloud, and have students repeat it. If necessary, encourage students to use this language when they do the activity.

> **Teaching tip** Make sure students understand the meaning of *relating an issue to the audience*. Explain or elicit that *relating* means *connecting*. Elicit an example of this for each of the issues in Exercise A before students work in groups.

- Ask for a volunteer to read the model language aloud, completing it with his or her own ideas.
- Give groups about 10 minutes to discuss their opinions.
- Walk around the classroom, helping students as necessary.
- Ask for a few volunteers to share their responses with the class.

② Supporting opinions
Page 59

> ### Notes
>
> **Useful language**
>
> **anecdote** a short, personal story often used to provide an example
>
> **obvious** easily recognized or understood
>
> **social group** a group of people with something in common, for example, interests or degree of wealth
>
> **to supervise** to be in charge of people's work or behavior

A ◉ Track 18

- Read the instructions aloud.
- Give students time to read the information individually. Encourage them to ask their classmates to explain any unfamiliar language. Then go over any language students still don't understand.
- Give students about two minutes to choose their guesses.
- Play the audio program once or twice as needed and have students check their guesses.
- Confirm answers by calling on students to say the correct pieces of information.

> ### Answers
>
> 1. **Alex:**
>   Some teens spend up to $100 a month on clothes.
>   Paying attention to fashion negatively affects schoolwork.
>   Differences between social groups are less obvious.
>
> 2. **Elena:**
>   Many kids think it's OK to share personal information.
>   Supervising kids' Internet use can help parents worry less.
>   It's a way to do something together with your kids.
>
> 3. **Lisa:**
>   Only 10 percent of people volunteer.
>   It's a valuable opportunity to get work experience.
>   A friend had trouble finding a job.

B

- Have students form pairs.
- Read the instructions aloud.
- Call on a student to read the written example aloud.
- Give pairs about five minutes to write their opinions and information.

> **Teaching tip** If students need ideas, tell them to look back at the issues on pages 56 and 57 in their Student's Books.

- Walk around the classroom, helping students as necessary.

C

- Combine pairs to form groups of four.
- Read the instructions aloud.
- Read the language in the box aloud, and have students repeat it. If necessary, encourage students to use this language when they do the activity.
- Point out the model language to help students get started.
- Give groups about 10 minutes to share their opinions and supporting information. Remind students to say whether they agree or disagree with the opinions.
- Walk around the classroom, helping students as necessary.
- To finish, lead the class in a mini debate about one of the issues. Have students choose an issue that many of them feel strongly about. Then ask students to share and support their opinions on the topic.

Organization focus

① Chris's persuasive presentation
Page 60

> ### Notes
>
> **Useful language**
>
> **to destroy** to damage or ruin
>
> **persuasive** able to convince someone to do or believe something
>
> **vegetarian** a person who does not eat meat

A

- Have students form pairs.
- Tell students to open to page 60 in their Student's Books, but have them cover Exercises B and C and page 61. Tell them to look only at the picture while you read the instructions and questions aloud.
- Give pairs about one minute to discuss the picture.
- Walk around the classroom, helping students as necessary.
- Ask for a few volunteers to share their responses with the class.

> ### Possible answers
>
> The issue is diet / natural foods / eating vegetables / being a vegetarian.
>
> He feels that people should eat healthy food / more vegetables.

- Tell students they are going to find out more details about Chris's opinion in this lesson and in the next lesson of the unit.

B

- Have students uncover their books.
- Read the instructions aloud.
- Have students look at the brainstorming notes and at the outline on page 61.
- Give students about two minutes to check the eight topics included in the outline.
- Go over the answers with the whole class.

> **Answers**
>
> Supporting information about cost
> A statement relating the issue to the audience
> My opposing opinion
> Statements to persuade the audience
> Supporting information about health
> The reasons for my opinion
> A summary of my opinion and the reasons
> Supporting information about helping the environment

C

> **Teaching tip** You may want to have students do this exercise in pairs, so they can help each other and share ideas.

- Read the instructions aloud.
- Give students time to read the notes. Explain any unfamiliar language.
- Give students about three minutes to complete the outline.
- Walk around the classroom, helping students as necessary.
- If students have been working individually, have them compare their answers in pairs.

2 Chris's outline 💿 Track 19
Page 61

> **Notes**
>
> **Useful language**
> **disease** a serious illness
> **industry** the companies and activities involved in the production of goods for sale

- Read the instructions aloud.
- Play the audio program and have students follow along with the outline.
- Check answers by reading through the outline aloud and calling on students to say the missing information.

> **Answers**
>
> I.   B. 2. Everyone should become a vegetarian.
> I.   C. 3. helps the environment
> II. A. 3. I lost five kilos, have more energy, feel great
> II. B. 1. meat is most expensive part of diet
> II. C. 2. about 25 percent of rain forest destroyed in Central America since 1960
> III. B. 2. wasn't easy, but made the right choice, and hope you will, too

Presentation focus

1 Introduction
Pages 62 and 63

> **Teaching tip** Before doing this lesson, you may want to encourage students to review the vocabulary and language presented in Unit 5. Hand out a copy of the Unit 5 **Language summary** (Teacher's Manual page 56) to each student in the class. Alternatively, refer students to the appropriate sections in their Student's Books if they need help completing the tasks.

- Tell students they are now going to focus on each section of Chris's presentation separately.
- Read the instructions aloud.
- Read the bullet points aloud. If necessary, remind students that the missing words in the presentation can all be found on pages 58 to 61.
- Give students about two minutes to read and complete the introduction.
- Walk around the classroom, helping students as necessary.

2 Body
Pages 62 and 63

- Read the instructions aloud.
- Call on a student to read the bullet points aloud.
- Give students about three minutes to read and complete the body.
- Walk around the classroom, helping students as necessary.

3 Conclusion
Pages 62 and 63

- Read the instructions aloud.
- Ask for a volunteer to read the bullet points and the model language aloud.
- Give students about two minutes to read and complete the conclusion.
- Walk around the classroom, helping students as necessary.

④ Chris's presentation 💿 Track 19
Pages 62 and 63

- Read the instructions aloud.
- Play the audio program and have students check their answers.
- Elicit the answers and write the correct answers on the board for students' reference.

Answers

Introduction: opinion, saves, helps
Body: fact, According, experience, know, article, read
Conclusion: diet, environment, enjoy

> **Teaching tip** You may want to finish by having students give their opinions on Chris's presentation. Write questions on the board, and have students discuss them in pairs or small groups. For example:
> *Do you agree with Chris? Why or why not?*
> *What do you think is Chris's strongest reason?*
> *Can you think of any other reasons?*
> *Would you ever stop eating meat? Why or why not?*

Presentation skills focus

① Emphasizing an opposing opinion
Page 64

Warm-up

- Books closed. Ask students to think back to Chris's presentation about eating meat. Ask how he began his presentation. Try to elicit from students that Chris began by mentioning an activity that is the opposite of his own main point or opinion. If necessary, have students open to page 63 in their Student's Books and look again at the presentation.
- Ask students, *Why did Chris begin his presentation that way?* Establish with students that it is because it helps the audience identify with Chris as being similar to them, and it helps to make his own topic and opinion more dramatic and interesting.
- Tell students that a persuasive presentation is often much more interesting and memorable when the presenter first mentions a common point of view, then clearly gives an opposite opinion.

A 💿 Track 20

- Tell students to open to page 64 in their Student's Books.
- Read the information at the top of the page aloud.
- Read the instructions aloud.
- Play the audio program and have students listen to the way the words in bold are emphasized.

B 💿 Track 21

- Read the instructions aloud.

- Give students time to read the partial sentences. Explain any unfamiliar language.
- Point out the example answer.
- Play the audio program once or twice as needed.
- Have students compare answers in pairs before you go over the answers with the class.

Answers

1. However, I believe
2. But in my opinion
3. But I feel strongly
4. However, in my opinion

- Ask for a volunteer to read the presentation tip aloud.

> **Teaching tip** You may want to model the presentation tip by reading a sentence from Exercise B and using gestures.

② Your turn
Page 65

> ### Notes
> **Useful language**
> **ethanol** fuel made from corn

A 💿 Track 22

- Read the instructions aloud.
- Give students about three minutes to read the example passage.
- Point out the example answer.
- Play the audio program once or twice as needed.
- Have students compare answers in pairs before you go over the answers with the class.

Answers

However, I feel **strongly**
But **I** don't believe
In **my** opinion
I think

- Play the audio program one more time. Tell students to listen to how the emphasized word sounds in the context of the phrase in which it is used.

B

- Have students form pairs.
- Read the instructions aloud.
- Give students about three minutes to take turns reading the passage. Have students stand, and encourage them to use their voices to emphasize the words. Remind them to follow the presentation tip on page 64. Encourage them to also use the presentation skills they learned in earlier units (for example, making eye contact with the audience).
- Walk around the classroom, helping students as necessary.

C

- Have students stay in their pairs from Exercise B.
- Read the instructions aloud.
- Give students about five minutes to think of an issue and write their information.
- Walk around the classroom, helping students as necessary.

D

- Have students form pairs.
- Read the instructions aloud.
- Point out the model language to help students get started.
- Tell students to read their sentences silently and underline any words they can emphasize.
- Have students take turns sharing their opinions. Have students stand, and remind them to use emphasis and to follow the presentation tip on page 64. Encourage them to also use the presentation skills they learned in earlier units (for example, making eye contact with the audience).
- Walk around the classroom, helping students as necessary.
- When students finish, tell them that they are now ready to begin planning their own persuasive presentations.

Present yourself!

1 Brainstorming
Page 66

- Read the assignment in the box at the top of the page aloud.
- Read the instructions aloud.
- Give students time to choose an issue they feel strongly about. If they need help doing this, refer them to pages 56 and 57 in their Student's Books for ideas.
- Have students complete the brainstorming map. Remind them not to write complete sentences. They should brainstorm as much information as possible about their issues and make brief notes.
- Walk around the classroom, helping students as necessary.
- If students need help, refer them to the example brainstorming notes on page 60 (Exercise B) in their Student's Books. Alternatively, have students watch while you draw a brainstorming map with notes about one of your opinions on the board. Then review the brainstorming map with the students.

2 Organizing
Page 67

Teaching tip Depending on your available class time, you may want to have students start this activity in class and finish it as homework.

- Read the instructions aloud.
- Have students read the topics in the outline.
- Give students time to think of a presentation title and complete the outline.
- Walk around the classroom, helping students as necessary.

Teaching tip If students need more help organizing their outlines, you may want to collect the outlines and give written feedback on them to the students.

- Have students make their final notes on note cards. Remind them that they should speak from abbreviated notes written on note cards, and should not read out their presentations word for word.
- Remind students to practice their presentations.

Teaching tip If time allows, you may want to have students form pairs or groups and take turns practicing their presentations in class. Suggest that students ask a classmate to time the length of their presentations, and encourage them to make suggestions to help improve their classmates' presentations.

3 Presenting
Page 67

Teaching tip Depending on your class size, you will need to determine the best format (group or whole class) and time limit for students' presentations.

- Read the instructions aloud.
- Explain the format and time limit for students' presentations (see *Teaching tip* above). Make sure students understand that they will be expected to use the language and presentation skills they learned in Unit 5, as well as any appropriate language and skills they have learned in the course so far.
- If you plan to have students use the **Outline worksheet** and **Peer evaluation form**, or if you plan to use the **Assessment form** during students' presentations, be sure to make the appropriate number of copies before students begin their presentations.
- When students finish their presentations, have them complete the **Self-evaluation** on page 84 in their Student's Books.

Unit 5	Teacher's Manual page
Language summary	56
Outline worksheet	62
Peer evaluation form	64
Assessment form	65

6 In the news

Overview

In this unit, students talk about current events and news stories they are interested in. They compare their news habits with classmates' and practice introducing and narrating news stories. In preparation for their own presentations about a news story, students look at brainstorming notes, complete a presentation outline, and listen to a model presentation about a news story. They then practice leading group discussions and, finally, choose a news story and prepare and give their own presentations about it.

Lesson	Activities
Topic focus	Talking about news headlines; words to describe news stories
Language focus	Introducing news stories; talking about details in news stories
Organization focus	Focusing on brainstorming ideas and creating an outline for a presentation about a news story
Presentation focus	Focusing on the introduction, body, and conclusion of a presentation; listening to a model presentation about a news story: *Worlds Apart*
Presentation skills focus	Leading a group discussion; encouraging audience participation
Present yourself!	Researching a news story; creating an outline; giving a presentation about the news story

Topic focus

① News headlines
Page 68

Teaching tip Some students may not follow the news regularly and may have trouble choosing news stories to discuss. If possible, when you begin this unit, bring to class a variety of newspapers and magazines to help students find news stories they are interested in.

Notes

Useful language

Amazonian tribe a large group of related families who share the same language and culture, and who live in South America near the Amazon River and rain forest

breakthrough a major discovery or advance, usually in science or technology

executive a person in a high management position in a company

extinction a situation in which a type of animal, plant, or tribe of people is totally destroyed so that it doesn't exist anymore

headline the words printed at the top of a newspaper story that tell what the story is about

record level the highest level ever

Warm-up

- Books closed. Ask students to tell you what topics or events have been in the news recently, either in their own country or in the world. Write the news topics on the board and ask students to tell you any details they know about them. Alternatively, you can ask students questions about their news habits, and whether they get their news online, from TV, in a newspaper, or in a magazine.
- Tell students that in this unit they will discuss news stories and have the opportunity to present news stories to their classmates.

A

- Have students form pairs.
- Tell students to open to page 68 in their Student's Books.
- Have students look at the pictures while you read the instructions aloud.
- Read the model language aloud and elicit ideas to complete the sentence.
- Give pairs about two minutes to discuss their ideas.
- Walk around the classroom, helping students as necessary.
- Ask for a few volunteers to say what they think the stories are about.

Possible answers

1. air safety, the cost of air travel
2. doing business, top corporations
3. global warming, the environment
4. cultural traditions, South American Indians
5. the space shuttle, space travel
6. gasoline prices, finding more oil

B

- Read the instructions aloud.
- Call on individual students to read the headlines aloud. Explain any unfamiliar language.
- Give students about three minutes to match the headlines to the pictures.
- Walk around the classroom, helping students as necessary.
- Go over the answers with the whole class.

Answers

1. e   2. g   3. f   4. a   5. b   6. c

C

- Have students stay in their pairs from Exercise A.
- Read the instructions aloud.
- Call on a few students to read the model language aloud, completing it with their own ideas.
- Give students about three minutes to discuss their answers.
- Walk around the classroom, helping students as necessary.
- Ask for a few volunteers to share their responses with the class.

② The news and you
Page 69

Notes

Useful language

astonishing very surprising or amazing
disturbing worrying or upsetting
heartwarming inspiring feelings of happiness or contentment, usually because people are being kind
moving causing strong emotions like sadness or sympathy
shocking extremely surprising
thought-provoking causing you to think seriously about a topic or an issue
timely happening at the best or most appropriate time

A

- Tell students they will now have a chance to discuss their news habits.
- Read the instructions aloud.
- Give students time to read and answer the questions individually.
- Have students compare answers in pairs.
- To finish, take a class poll to find out the most popular answers. Read the survey questions aloud, and have students raise their hands to answer. Tally the results on the board.

B

- Read the instructions aloud.
- Point out the written example in the chart.
- Give students about five minutes to complete the chart.
- Walk around the classroom, helping students as necessary.
- Have students form pairs and share their stories.

C

- Have pairs combine to form groups of four.
- Read the instructions aloud.
- Read the *Words to describe news stories* in the box aloud and have students repeat them.
- Ask for volunteers to give synonyms and examples to help explain the vocabulary. Then go over any vocabulary students still don't understand.
- Call on two students to read the model language aloud.
- Give groups about 10 minutes to share their stories. Remind them to react using the new vocabulary as shown in the model language.
- Walk around the classroom, helping students as necessary.
- To finish, lead a brief discussion about the news stories students bring up. Have volunteers from the groups share their stories with the class, and have the rest of the class react using the new vocabulary.

Language focus

❶ Introducing news stories
Page 70

Notes

Useful language

to summarize to recap the most important facts of a story

trend a gradual change or development over time

Warm-up

- Books closed. Briefly introduce a news story to the students, for example, *Yesterday I read a really heartwarming article in the L.A. Times newspaper about a poor family that won 10 million dollars in the lottery.* Now ask students what information you gave them related to the article. If they have trouble telling you, you may want to write on the board:
  When:
  Source:
  Topic:
  My reaction:
- Students can then fill in (or tell you) the information:
  When: *yesterday*
  Source: *L.A. Times newspaper*
  Topic: *poor family won the lottery*
  My reaction: *heartwarming*
- Tell students that in this lesson they are going to practice introducing a news article and explaining the details.

A

- Tell students to open to page 70 in their Student's Books.
- Have students look at the pictures while you read the instructions aloud.
- Ask for volunteers to read the headlines above the pictures aloud.
- Have students discuss what they know about the stories in pairs.
- Elicit responses from a few students.

B 💿 Track 23

- Read the instructions aloud.
- Give students about one minute to read the information. Explain any unfamiliar language.
- Point out the example answer.
- Play the audio program once or twice as needed.
- Go over the answers with the whole class.

Answers

Mei (*M*): magazine, population trends, give my reaction

Jeff (*J*): TV, modern lifestyles, summarize main points

Luis (*L*): Internet, fast-food warnings, share your opinion

C

- Have students form pairs.
- Read the instructions aloud.
- Read the language in the box aloud, and have students repeat it. If necessary, encourage students to use this language when they do the activity.
- Ask what three things should be included in their introductions (*news source*, *topic*, *preview of the presentation*).
- Point out the model language to help students get started.
- Give students time to look back at their stories on page 69. Have them practice introducing the stories individually and encourage them to write notes to help them if they need to.
- Give pairs about five minutes to introduce their stories.
- Walk around the classroom, helping students as necessary.
- Ask for a few volunteers to introduce their news stories to the class.

❷ The details
Page 71

Notes

Useful language

billion 1,000,000,000

birthrate the number of children born during a period of time

demand a need

overwhelmed feeling unable to cope because one has too many things to do

A 💿 Track 24

- Tell students that they will now hear details of the three stories on page 70.
- Read the instructions aloud.
- Call on individual students to read the answer choices aloud. Explain any unfamiliar language.

Teaching tip For lower-level classes, have students do a prelistening prediction activity. Have them guess which details will be included in the stories.

- Play the audio program once or twice as needed.
- Go over the answers with the whole class.

Answers

1. **Mei:** Some Asian countries have very low birthrates.
2. **Jeff:** Many women feel overwhelmed by the demands of work and family.
3. **Luis:** The government may put warnings on unhealthy foods.

B 💿 Track 24

- Read the instructions aloud.
- Ask for volunteers to read the answer choices aloud. Explain (or have students explain to their classmates) any unfamiliar language.
- Play the audio program once or twice as needed.
- Check answers by reading the details and calling on students to say *true* or *false*.

> **Answers**
>
> 1. **Mei:** false   2. **Jeff:** true   3. **Luis:** true

❸ Reality or fiction?
Page 71

> **Notes**
>
> **Useful language**
> **elderly** of old age
> **in place of** instead of; as a replacement for
> **to look after** to take care of
> **robot** a machine that can do the work of humans

A

- Read the instructions aloud.
- Point out the written example in the chart.
- Give students about three minutes to complete the chart individually. Encourage them to think of (or create) unusual, funny, or interesting stories.
- Walk around the classroom, helping students as necessary.

B

- Have students form groups of three or four.
- Read the instructions aloud.
- Read the language in the box aloud, and have students repeat it. Encourage students to use this language, and the language on page 70, when they do the activity.
- Point out the model language to help students get started.
- Give students about five minutes to share their news stories. Remind them to first introduce the story, and then talk about the details.
- Walk around the classroom, helping students as necessary.
- Ask for a few volunteers to share their news stories with the class.

Organization focus

❶ Mari's news story
Page 72

> **Notes**
>
> **Useful language**
> **arms** weapons
> **charity** an organization that gives money, food, or help to those who need it
> **nongovernmental** private, not related to the government
> **poverty** the condition of not having enough money to pay for basic needs

A

- Have students form pairs.
- Tell students to open to page 72 in their Student's Books, but have them cover Exercises B and C and page 73. Tell them to look only at the picture while you read the instructions and questions aloud.
- Give pairs about one minute to discuss the picture.
- Walk around the classroom, helping students as necessary.
- Ask for a few volunteers to share their responses with the class.

> **Possible answers**
>
> The topic is education in Africa / around the world.
> The story is astonishing / heartwarming / shocking.

- Tell students they are going to find out more details of Mari's news story in this lesson and in the next lesson of the unit.

B

- Have students uncover their books.
- Read the instructions aloud.
- Have students look at the brainstorming notes and at the outline on page 73.
- Give students about two minutes to check the nine topics included in the outline.
- Ask for volunteers to say the topics they checked.

> **Answers**
>
> A question for the audience to think about
> A preview of the presentation
> Details about world poverty
> An invitation for audience members to share their views
> My reaction to the news story
> Details about what is being done
> An introduction to the news story
> A surprising fact about the topic
> Details about education

c

- Read the instructions aloud.
- Give students time to read the notes. Explain any unfamiliar language.
- Give students about three minutes to complete the outline.
- Walk around the classroom, helping students as necessary.
- If students have been working individually, have them compare their answers in pairs.

2 Mari's outline 💿 Track 25
Page 73

> **Notes**
>
> **Useful language**
>
> **corporation** a business that is legally separate from those who run it
>
> **view** an opinion

- Read the instructions aloud.
- Play the audio program and have students follow along with the outline.
- Check answers by reading through the outline aloud and calling on individual students to say the missing information.

> **Answers**
>
> I.   B.   Half the world's population lives on less than $2 a day.
> I.   C.   2.   the topic: poverty in the world
> I.   D.   1.   outline main points
> I.   D.   3.   share your opinion at end
> II. A.   2.   one in two children lives in poverty
> II. B.   2. $10 billion is enough to put every child in school, but is less than one percent of what world spends on arms
> II. C.   1.   nongovernmental organizations and charities are helping
> III. A.   1.   story is shocking, moving

Presentation focus

1 Introduction
Pages 74 and 75

- Tell students they are now going to focus on each section of Mari's presentation separately.
- Read the instructions aloud.
- Read the bullet points and the model language aloud. If necessary, remind students that the missing words in the presentation can all be found on pages 70 to 73.
- Give students about two minutes to read and complete the introduction.
- Walk around the classroom, helping students as necessary.

2 Body
Pages 74 and 75

> **Notes**
>
> **Useful language**
>
> **glad** happy
>
> **statistic** a numerical fact or measurement

- Read the instructions aloud.
- Ask for a volunteer to read the bullet point aloud.
- Give students about three minutes to read and complete the body.
- Walk around the classroom, helping students as necessary.

3 Conclusion
Pages 74 and 75

- Read the instructions aloud.
- Ask for a volunteer to read the bullet points and the model language aloud.
- Give students about two minutes to read and complete the conclusion.
- Walk around the classroom, helping students as necessary.

4 Mari's presentation 💿 Track 25
Pages 74 and 75

- Read the instructions aloud.
- Play the audio program and have students check their answers.
- Ask for volunteers to read sections of the presentation aloud, inserting the missing words.
- Write the correct answers on the board for students' reference.

Answers

Introduction: Half, read, talked, points, share
Body: According, on, looked, went, say
Conclusion: shocking, charity, make

Teaching tip You may want to finish by having students give their reactions to Mari's news story. Write questions on the board, and have students discuss them in pairs or small groups. For example:
Is your reaction to this article similar to Mari's?
Which facts and statistics in the article are the most surprising to you?
What other things do you think we can do to help people living in poverty?

Presentation skills focus

1 Leading a group discussion
Page 76

Warm-up

- Books closed. Ask students how Mari ended her presentation. Elicit or explain that she ended it with an audience discussion of what can be done to help people in poverty. Tell students that often, a presenter will leave time for an open discussion at the end of the presentation, especially when the presentation concerns an important issue about which people have different ideas or opinions.

▼

💿 Track 26
- Tell students to open to page 76 in their Student's Books.
- Read the information at the top of the page aloud.
- Read the instructions aloud. Make sure students understand that *open* means *begin*, and *close* means *end*.
- Read the sentences aloud, and have students repeat them.
- Point out the example answer.
- Give students about five minutes to complete the sections.
- Play the audio program and have students check their answers.

- Go over the answers with the whole class.
- Point out that all the sentences used to continue a discussion are questions.

Answers

Open:
Now I'd like to hear your views.
I'd like to invite you to share your ideas.
Now it's your turn to voice your opinions.
Continue:
Can anyone add to that?
Do you all agree?
What do you think, Mark?
Close:
We've heard a lot of great ideas today.
That's all the time we have. Thanks for sharing your views.
Thank you for participating today.

- Ask for a volunteer to read the presentation tip aloud.

2 Your turn
Page 77

Notes

Useful language
up to the responsibility of

A

- Read the instructions aloud.
- Give students about five minutes to read the discussion and underline the sentences.
- Walk around the classroom, helping students as necessary.
- Check answers by asking for volunteers to say which sentences they underlined.

Answers

Now it's your turn to voice your opinions.
Do you all agree?
Can anyone add to that?
Well, everyone, that's all the time we have. Thanks for sharing your views.

B

- Have students form groups of three.
- Read the instructions aloud.
- Tell groups to decide which roles students will play: Mari, Jack, or Eva.
- Give groups about five minutes to read the discussion. Encourage students to look down and remember their line, then look up and make eye contact when they speak to their group members. Remind groups to change roles twice.

- Walk around the classroom, helping students as necessary.
- Ask for volunteer groups to stand and present their discussions for the class.

C

- Read the instructions aloud. Make sure students understand that they can use any of the expressions from page 76, as long as they use them in the appropriate places to open, continue, and close the discussion.
- Give students about three minutes to read and complete the discussion.
- Walk around the classroom, helping students as necessary.

Possible answers

Classmate 1 (first turn):

Now I'd like to hear your views.

I'd like to invite you to share your ideas.

Now it's your turn to voice your opinions.

Classmate 1 (second and third turns):

Can anyone add to that?

Do you all agree?

What do you think, (name)?

Classmate 1 (fourth turn):

We've heard a lot of great ideas today.

That's all the time we have. Thanks for sharing your views.

Thank you for participating today.

D

- Have students form the same groups they worked in for Exercise B.
- Tell groups to decide which roles students will play: Classmates 1, 2, or 3.
- Read the instructions aloud.
- Give students about five minutes to read the discussion. Encourage them to look down and remember their line, then look up and make eye contact when they speak to their group members. Remind groups to change roles twice.
- Walk around the classroom, helping students as necessary.
- Call on a few groups to stand and present their discussions for the class.
- When students finish, tell them that they are now ready to begin planning their own news story presentations.

Present yourself!

❶ Brainstorming
Page 78

> **Teaching tip** As this presentation requires students to do research on a news story, plan to begin the brainstorming process in class. Then allot the remaining class time for students' research, and assign the rest of the research as homework.

- Read the assignment in the box at the top of the page aloud.
- Read the instructions aloud.
- Give students time to choose a story. If they need help doing this, refer them to pages 68 and 69 in their Student's Books for ideas.
- Have students complete their research.
- Remind students not to write complete sentences. They should brainstorm as much information as possible and make brief notes.
- Walk around the classroom, helping students as necessary.
- If students need help, refer them to the example brainstorming notes on page 72 (Exercise B) in their Student's Books. Alternatively, have the class choose an example news story. Then elicit some possible details for each brainstorming topic and write them on the board.

❷ Organizing
Page 79

> **Teaching tip** Depending on your available class time, you may want to have students start this activity in class and finish it as homework.

- Read the instructions aloud.
- Have students read the topics in the outline.
- Give students time to think of a presentation title and complete the outline.
- Walk around the classroom, helping students as necessary.

> **Teaching tip** If students need more help organizing their outlines, you may want to collect the outlines and give written feedback on them to the students.

- Have students make their final notes on note cards. Remind them that they should speak from abbreviated notes written on note cards, and should not read out their presentations word for word.
- Remind students to practice their presentations.

Teaching tip If time allows, you may want to have students form pairs or groups and take turns practicing their presentations in class. Suggest that students ask a classmate to time the length of their presentations, and encourage them to make suggestions to help improve their classmates' presentations.

❸ Presenting
Page 79

Teaching tip Depending on your class size, you will need to determine the best format (group or whole class) and time limit for students' presentations.

- Read the instructions aloud.
- Explain the format and time limit for students' presentations (see *Teaching tip* above). Make sure students understand that they will be expected to use the language and presentation skills they learned in Unit 6, as well as any appropriate language and skills they have learned in the course so far.

- If you plan to have students use the **Outline worksheet** and **Peer evaluation form**, or if you plan to use the **Assessment form** during students' presentations, be sure to make the appropriate number of copies before students begin their presentations.
- When students finish their presentations, have them complete the **Self-evaluation** on page 85 in their Student's Books.

Unit 6	Teacher's Manual page
Language summary	57
Outline worksheet	63
Peer evaluation form	64
Assessment form	65

Language summaries

Unit 1 Language summary

Personal mottoes

A candle loses none of its light by lighting another candle.

A smile can brighten someone's darkest day.

Aim for the impossible, and you'll achieve the improbable.

Always do what you are afraid to do.

Choose a job you love, and you'll never have to work a day in your life.

If at first you don't succeed, try, try again.

Just jump.

Laughter is the best medicine.

Life is not a rehearsal.

Life is what you make of it.

Look before you leap.

Make every day count.

Make new friends, but keep the old. One is silver, and the other is gold.

Money makes the world go around.

Never stop learning.

People who don't make mistakes don't make anything.

Shared joy is double joy.

The best things in life are free.

Variety is the spice of life.

Personal values

being kind to others

enjoying life

enjoying your work

following dreams

getting an education

keeping good relationships

taking risks

valuing money

Connecting with the audience

If you're like me . . .

I'm sure you'll agree that . . .

Previewing a presentation

Today I'm going to share . . .

Then I'll go on to talk about . . .

Finally, I'll tell you . . .

Relating a motto to a past experience

This motto has helped me a lot.

I've relied on this motto several times.

I try to live my life by this motto when I can.

Talking about how a motto helps you in life

My motto helps me get through difficult times.

It makes me appreciate others.

It also reminds me that change is good.

Expressing a wish for the audience that relates to your motto

Remember that you can make a difference, too.

Talking about personal values

. . . is one of my personal values.

Some other things I value include . . .

Explaining the meaning of a motto

This means that
In other words, it's important to enjoy life.
That is,

For instance, when I . . .

For example, three months ago . . .

Unit 2 Language summary

Survey topics

career goals

cell phone use

exercise habits

news preferences

part-time jobs

shopping habits

TV-viewing habits

How much time do you spend on homework?

How often do you buy new clothes?

What do you think is the most important feature of a part-time job?

What do you use your cell phone for the most?

What do you value the most in your life?

Would you say that your schoolwork is too difficult, or not difficult enough?

Survey questions

Do you think you can change the world?

Do your parents support you financially?

Stating general information about a topic

Experts say that young people's . . .   **These days,** young people . . .

Describing a survey

| **I did a survey to find out about**
 I conducted a survey about | eating habits. |

| **I interviewed**
 I surveyed
 The group included | ten university students | **aged** 18 **to** 22.
 between the ages of 18 **and** 22. |

Reporting survey results

Two (people) **said** they watch TV.

Three out of ten (people) **said** they own a bicycle.

Ten percent (of students) **said** they work part-time.

| **One-quarter**
 One-third
 Half
 Two-thirds
 Three-quarters | **(of the** students)
 (of the people **surveyed)** | **said** they eat fruit. |

Summarizing results

The results of this survey show that . . .

Giving a conclusion and recommendation

From this survey, I can conclude that . . .

I think the government **should** . . .

Explaining visual aids

| **As this** | **pie chart**
 graph
 table
 Venn diagram | **shows,**
 illustrates,
 explains,
 makes clear, | 80 percent of people said they eat meat. |

Unit 3 Language summary

Types of vacations
beach resort vacation

historic sightseeing tour

luxury cruise

outdoor adventure

rain forest ecotour

wildlife safari

Accommodations
bed-and-breakfast

bungalow

cabin

five-star resort

luxury hotel

tent

youth hostel

Activities
do outdoor sports

eat at old restaurants

go on an island cruise / a night safari

hike through the jungle

learn about animals / architecture / art / plants

meet people

relax

sightsee

spend time shopping

visit the countryside

watch the sunset

Asking about the audience's travel preferences
Are you fed up with crowded airports?

Are you looking for your dream vacation?

Are you tired of working on weekends?

Do you love / need / want sandy beaches?

Describing the type of people who would enjoy the vacation
This (vacation) is perfect for people who love shopping.

Talking about vacation destinations
It's situated   in the north of the country.

Estonia **is located**   in Eastern Europe.

It's one of the most beautiful cities in Europe.

It's known for its
It offers   stunning views.

Talking about activities and accommodations
You can hike through the jungle.

	be able to	
You'll	**have a chance to**	go on a safari.
	have an opportunity to	

You'll stay in a luxury hotel.

You'll spend two **nights in a** cabin.

Explaining the cost and length of stay
The cost is $400 **for** three **nights**.

Summarizing what a vacation includes
This vacation includes five nights in a luxury resort.

Unit 4 Language summary

Process topics

consumer products

the human body

nature

science and technology

world cultures

How Does Thunder Happen?

How Hybrid Cars Work

How Text Messaging Works

The Secrets of Ice-Cream Making

The Sleep Cycle

Tsunami Formation

Understanding Digital Photography

Understanding the Internet

University Systems in the United States and Europe

The U.S. Election Process

Why Do Volcanoes Erupt?

Process presentation titles

The Art of the Japanese Tea Ceremony

Herbal Tea: A Growing Business

How Are Rainbows Formed?

How Do People Hear?

Sharing an interesting fact about a process

Did you know that . . . ?

Many people don't know that . . .

A preview of a presentation

In this	**presentation, talk,**	**I'll**	**explain discuss go over**	how the Internet works.

Inviting audience questions

Feel free to interrupt me if you have questions.

If you have questions, please ask them at any time.

I'll be happy to take your questions when I'm finished.

I'll take questions after the presentation.

Please hold your questions until the end.

Please stop me at any time if you have questions.

Explaining a process

The	**first second next final**	**stage is** the light sleep stage.

In the first stage, reporters investigate facts.

This is when During this stage, At this point,	stories are researched.

Reviewing the stages of a process

That completes the sleep cycle.

Giving recommendations for further research

For those of you who'd like to find out more, I recommend . . .

If you'd like to learn more, you can . . .

Unit 5 Language summary

Issues categories

education
the environment
human relationships
lifestyle and health
media and technology
society and politics

Issues

fast food
global warming
Internet use
marriage
medical research
raising children
recycling
school uniforms
taxes

university tuition
violence on TV
volunteer work

Opinions

Advertising aimed at children should be banned.
All cars should have hybrid engines.
All high school students should wear school uniforms.
All university students should do volunteer work.
Everyone should learn English.
Only very wealthy people should pay taxes.
People should wait until age 30 to get married.
People shouldn't eat meat.
Recycling should be required by law.
The Internet makes life better.
Traveling is more educational than going to school.
Watching TV harms young people.

Relating an issue

Many of you say that TV is educational.

Most people believe that water should be free.

We all enjoy seeing new places.

Expressing an opposing opinion

However, I think / believe that all cars should have hybrid engines.

But in my opinion, recycling should be required by law.

But I feel strongly that watching TV harms young people.

Supporting an opinion

Did you know that some teens spend up to $100 a month on clothes?

It's a fact that half the world's population has cell phones.

According to **experts, researchers,** 70% of children use the Internet.

An article I read said that meat products cost three times as much as an equal amount of vegetables.

In my experience, volunteer work is very rewarding.

Here's an example that supports my opinion.

Summarizing an opinion and the reasons

In conclusion, I believe . . .

Making a statement to persuade the audience

I know it's not easy to . . .
I made the right choice, and I hope you will, too.

Unit 6 Language summary

News categories
business
entertainment
health
international
politics
science and technology
sports

Words to describe news stories
astonishing
disturbing
fascinating
heartwarming
moving
shocking
thought-provoking
timely

Sentences for leading a group discussion
Can anyone add to that?
Do you all agree?
I'd like to invite you to share your ideas.
Now I'd like to hear your views.
Now it's your turn to voice your opinions.
Thank you for participating today.
That's all the time we have. Thanks for sharing your views.
We've heard a lot of great ideas today.
What do you think?

Giving a question for the audience to think about
Think for a second.   Can you imagine . . . ?   Suppose you . . .

Sharing a surprising fact about the topic
You may be surprised to hear that . . .

Introducing a news story

I	read / saw / heard	a shocking	article / report / story	on	the Internet. / TV. / the radio.

It	looked at / talked about	poverty in the world.

First, / Today,	I'm going to	outline / summarize	the main points of the article / report / story.

Then, I'll	give you my reaction. / tell you how I feel about it.

At the end,	you'll have a chance to share your opinion. / I'll ask for your comments and opinions.

Talking about details in a news story

According to the article / report / story, many children live in poverty.

The article / report / story	**said / stated**	**that** many organizations are helping.

It went on to say that 27,000 children die every day from extreme poverty.

Reacting to a news story
I think this story is . . .   It made me feel . . .

Inviting audience members to share their views
Now I'd like to hear your views on . . .

Outline worksheets

Unit 1 Outline worksheet

Presenter: _____

A Motto for Life

I. Introduction

  A. A statement to connect with the audience

  _____

  B. The person's personal values

  _____

  _____

  C. A preview of the presentation

  _____

  _____

II. Body

  A. The person's motto

  _____

  B. The meaning

  _____

  _____

  C. Past experiences that relate to the person's motto

  _____

  _____

  _____

  _____

III. Conclusion

  A. How the motto helps the person in life

  _____

  _____

  B. A wish for the audience that relates to the person's motto

  _____

Something else I'd like to know about the topic: _____

_____

Unit 2 Outline worksheet

Presenter: _____

Young People Today

I. Introduction

   A. General information about the topic

     _____

     _____

   B. The aim of the survey

     _____

     _____

II. Body

   A. A description of the survey group

     _____

     _____

   B. A report of the survey results

     • the questions asked

     • the number of people and what they answered

     _____

     _____

     _____

     _____

     _____

     _____

     _____

III. Conclusion

   A. A summary of the results

     _____

     _____

   B. The person's conclusion and recommendation

     _____

     _____

Something else I'd like to know about the topic: _____

_____

Unit 3 Outline worksheet

Presenter: _____

Dream Vacation

I. **Introduction**

   A. Questions about the audience's travel preferences

    _____

    _____

   B. The name and type of vacation

    _____

   C. Who would enjoy it

    _____

II. **Body**

   A. The destination – the location, the description, the highlights

    _____

    _____

    _____

    _____

   B. The activities to do there

    _____

    _____

    _____

   C. The accommodations

    _____

    _____

III. **Conclusion**

   A. The cost and length of stay

    _____

    _____

   B. A summary of what the vacation includes

    _____

    _____

Something else I'd like to know about the topic: _____

_____

Unit 4 Outline worksheet

Presenter: _____

How the World Works

I. Introduction

  A. An interesting fact about the process

    _____

  B. A preview of the presentation

    • an introduction to the process

    _____

    • an invitation for audience questions

    _____

II. Body

  An explanation of the process

  • the stages and what happens

  _____

  _____

  _____

  _____

  _____

  _____

  _____

  _____

  _____

  _____

III. Conclusion

  A. A review of all the stages of the process

    _____

    _____

  B. Recommendations for further research

    _____

    _____

Something else I'd like to know about the topic: _____

_____

Unit 5 Outline worksheet

Presenter: _____

In My Opinion

I. Introduction

A. A statement relating the issue to the audience

_____

B. The person's opposing opinion

_____

C. The reasons for the person's opinion

_____

_____

II. Body

Information to support the person's opinion (supporting information)

• general information and facts

• examples and anecdotes

_____

_____

_____

_____

_____

_____

_____

_____

III. Conclusion

A. A summary of the person's opinion and the reasons

_____

_____

B. Statements to persuade the audience

_____

_____

Something else I'd like to know about the topic: _____

_____

_____

Unit 6 Outline worksheet

Presenter: _____

In the News

I. Introduction

   A. A question for the audience to think about

   _____

   B. A surprising fact about the topic

   _____

   _____

   C. An introduction to the news story

     • the news source: _____

     • the topic: _____

   D. A preview of the presentation

   _____

   _____

   _____

II. Body

   The details of the news story

   _____

   _____

   _____

   _____

   _____

III. Conclusion

   A. The person's reaction to the news story

   _____

   _____

   B. An invitation for audience members to share their views

   _____

   _____

Something else I'd like to know about the topic: _____

_____

_____

Peer evaluation form

Read each statement. Circle ☺, ☺, or ☹. Then write comments that will help your classmate improve next time.

Presenter: _____

Unit / Topic: _____

				Comments
The topic of the presentation was interesting.	☺	☺	☹	
The presentation had a clear introduction, body, and conclusion.	☺	☺	☹	
The presenter was relaxed, well-prepared, and confident.	☺	☺	☹	
The presenter spoke clearly and was easy to understand.	☺	☺	☹	
The presenter maintained good posture and made eye contact.	☺	☺	☹	
The presenter used the vocabulary and language from this unit effectively.	☺	☺	☹	
The presenter used the presentation skill from this unit effectively.	☺	☺	☹	

One thing that the presenter did well was _____

_____.

One suggestion that I have for the presenter is _____

_____.

Assessment form

Presenter: _____

Unit / Topic: _____

PREPARATION	Lowest				Highest
Presentation notes – written on note cards, brief, well-organized	1	2	3	4	5
Practice – student is relaxed, confident, well-prepared	1	2	3	4	5
Materials – visual aids or other materials prepared in advance, organized, easy to see	1	2	3	4	5
CONTENT					
Assignment – presentation is appropriate length, follows outline, uses language and skills from unit	1	2	3	4	5
Topic – relates to audience's needs and interests	1	2	3	4	5
Organization – introduction, body, and conclusion clear, easy to follow	1	2	3	4	5
DELIVERY					
Stage presence – student uses appropriate eye contact, posture, and relevant gestures	1	2	3	4	5
Language and voice – clear, easy to understand, grammatically correct, appropriate stress and intonation	1	2	3	4	5

TOTAL: _____ / 40

What the presenter did well

Suggestions

Student's Book audio scripts

Getting ready

Preparing to present Page 3

2. Presentation steps

B Track 2

Dan: Advice for planning a presentation? Sure, I've got a few hints. There are five things I like to do when I prepare a presentation. Number one: Choose a presentation topic. When choosing a presentation topic, think about your audience. Select something that will interest them. Number two: Brainstorm. You should write down as many topics and details as you can think of, and get all your ideas down on paper. Number three: Write an outline. For this, you should organize the main topics and details for the introduction, the body, and the conclusion of your presentation. Number four: Make presentation notes. Use note cards for these and write only brief phrases, not full sentences. And number five: Practice. Go over your presentation notes out loud, and be sure to time your presentation, to make sure it's not too long or short.

Introducing a classmate Page 5

2. Organizing

B Track 3

Dan: Hi, my name is Dan. Today I'd like to introduce our classmate Emma. I'm going to tell you about her hometown, family, and free-time activities. Emma was born in Taipei. However, she grew up in San Diego, California. She has a small family. Her parents live in Taipei, and she has an older brother who lives in California, too. He's 25 and works in a bank. When Emma has free time, she plays soccer. She's even on the university team! She also plays the guitar. Now you know a little about Emma, her hometown, family, and free-time activities. Thank you for listening.

Unit 1 A motto for life

Language focus Pages 10 and 11

1. Mottoes and their meanings

A, B Track 4

1. **Josh:** I think it's important to have goals in life, so following dreams is one of my personal values. Although I know we can't control everything that happens to us in life, I believe we have the power to make our own lives better and our dreams come true. That's why my motto is "Life is what you make of it." This means that people have more control over their lives than they think.

2. **Yumi:** I love trying all kinds of different things, and enjoying life is one of my personal values. For example, take food. I love Italian food, but I wouldn't want to

eat it every day. I would get tired of it pretty quickly. My motto is "Variety is the spice of life." In other words, life is much more interesting if you have lots of different experiences.

3. **Andy:** I know that risks are necessary to succeed, so taking risks is one of my personal values. I used to hate it when my English teacher asked me a question in front of the class. I was so afraid of making mistakes. But one day he taught me the motto, "People who don't make mistakes don't make anything." This means that mistakes are an important part of learning. For example, if you make a mistake in English class, you'll learn to do it right the next time.

2. Mottoes and experiences

A, B Track 5

1. **Josh:** My motto is "Life is what you make of it," and I try to live my life by this motto as much as possible. For instance, two years ago, I failed my university entrance exam. Of course I was disappointed, but then I remembered my motto. I decided to think about the future and work really hard to take the exam again. So, I focused on my weak areas, took extra classes, and did as many practice exams as I could. Then, last year, I passed the exam!

2. **Yumi:** My motto, "Variety is the spice of life," has helped me a lot. For example, it helped me when I started university. I thought about joining the same clubs that I'd belonged to in high school, but then I remembered my motto and decided to join new clubs. So, I made a list of clubs that I was interested in. I got information from other students about those clubs, and I met the managers of some of them. I decided to join three new clubs, and I'm really enjoying all of them!

3. **Andy:** My motto is "People who don't make mistakes don't make anything," and I've relied on this motto several times. For example, I've been playing the guitar since I was in elementary school. A few years ago, I was asked to join a band by my friend. At first, I thought I wasn't good enough to play for other people. But I thought of my motto and changed my mind. I joined the band and I loved it! I learned from my mistakes, I practiced even more and I started singing, too. I gained a lot more confidence in my ability. I'm so glad I decided to join the band.

Organization focus Page 13

2. Tim's outline

Presentation focus Page 14

4. Tim's presentation

Track 6

Tim: If you're like me, you enjoy helping people and making them feel good. Being kind to others is one of my personal values. Some other things I value include honesty, and my relationships with friends and family. Today I'm going to share my personal motto and explain its meaning. Then I'll go on to talk about some past experiences that relate to my motto. Finally, I'll tell you how my motto helps me in life.

My motto is "A candle loses none of its light by lighting another candle." In other words, when you light one candle with another, the first candle doesn't go out; it stays just as bright. This means that it doesn't take a lot of effort to be kind to others, and it makes us feel good.

I try to live my life by this motto as much as possible. For instance, a few years ago, I found a bag containing a wallet, camera, and other valuables on a park bench. There was a hotel card in the bag, so I took it straight to that hotel. In the hotel lobby, a young man, in a panic, was in the middle of telling the staff that he'd lost his bag somewhere. He was really pleased to see his bag, and was very grateful that I'd brought it to the hotel. He offered me some money as a reward, but I didn't accept it.

Recently I lost my wallet on the train, but luckily someone handed it in to the station lost-and-found office. I went to pick it up, and this time, I was the one feeling grateful. It really made my day.

My motto makes me appreciate help from others, and it helps me to be honest. It also reminds me that I can make the world a better place by doing something kind for someone else. Remember that you can be a candle, too, and it's easy to light many other candles each and every day. Thank you.

Unit 2 Young people today

Language focus Pages 22 and 23

1. Describing a survey

A, B Track 7

1. **Sun Hee:** Many adults say that young people these days spend too much time in front of the television. But is this really true? I wanted to know. So, I conducted a survey about teenagers' TV-viewing habits. I surveyed 16 teenagers, all aged 15 to 19. The group included nine girls and seven boys.

2. **Ken:** Experts say that in order to maintain good health, people should do some type of physical activity, such as walking or jogging, at least three times a week. I did a survey to find out about the exercise habits of young people. I interviewed 19 young adults between the ages of 18 and 24. The group included 10 men and 9 women.

3. **Paula:** Most university students think it's important to know what's going on in the world, and these days, there are more ways than ever to find out. But where do most young people get their news? I conducted a survey about young people's news preferences. The group included 12 university students aged 18 to 22. I interviewed six males and six females.

2. Survey results

A, B Track 8

1. **Sun Hee:** The first question I asked the teenagers was how many hours a week they watch TV. Some of the results were surprising. As this graph shows, 47 percent of the teens said they watch 20 or more hours a week! One-third of the teens surveyed said they watch 10 to 19 hours. That's still a lot of TV-watching. And only 20 percent, or one out of five, said they watch zero to nine hours a week.

2. **Ken:** First, I asked the group how often they exercise, and the results were interesting. As this pie chart explains, 28 percent said they do some kind of exercise every day. Good for them! 45 percent said they exercise a few times a week. That's still very good. One-quarter of the young adults surveyed said they only exercise once a week. And finally, two percent of the people said they exercise less than once a week.

3. **Paula:** For my first question, I asked university students where they get the news. As this graph makes clear, 20 percent said they read the newspaper. Only three percent said they listen to the radio. And what about TV? Well, only 10 percent of the people surveyed said they watch the TV news. So, what's the most popular news source? Well, two-thirds of the university students said they use the Internet to find out what's going on.

Organization focus Page 25

2. Hannah's outline

Presentation focus Page 26

4. Hannah's presentation

Track 9

Hannah: Experts say that young people's eating habits are worse than ever. These days, young people are buying more fast food than ever, too. Well, I did a survey to find out about the eating habits of university students, and I think you'll find the results very interesting.

For my survey, I interviewed 18 university students, aged 18 to 25. The group included 11 women and 7 men. Now I'd like to report the results of my survey. First I asked the students about their eating habits, and how healthy they think they are. Twenty-three percent said they were very healthy, and 25 percent answered they were pretty healthy. But here's the interesting part: Half of the university students said they have unhealthy eating habits. So, what are university students eating? Well, first I asked about healthy foods. As this chart shows, about 50 percent of the students said they eat at least one piece of fruit every day. But only one-third, or 33 percent of them, said they eat vegetables every day. Twenty percent of the students surveyed said they eat vegetables only once or twice a week! And what about unhealthy foods? Well, I asked about junk food and fast food, and as this graph illustrates, around two-thirds of the students surveyed said they eat junk food every day. As this table explains, 75 percent of the students surveyed said they eat fast food at least once a week! Only two students said they never, or almost never, eat fast food. The reason most students gave for eating fast food was that they are very busy, and fast food is quicker and more convenient for them than healthy food.

The results of this survey show that most university students do not have healthy eating habits. From this survey, I can conclude that university students don't have enough convenient and healthy food choices. They need more. I think university officials should make more healthy foods available to students on campus. Thank you.

Presentation skills focus Page 28

1. Explaining visual aids

B Track 10

1. **Woman:** As this graph explains, 20 percent of students said they want to study in the United States.

2. **Man:** As this pie chart illustrates, 25 percent of young people said they prefer pop music.

3. **Man:** As this Venn diagram shows, 33 percent of people said they watch movies online.

4. **Woman:** As this table makes clear, 20 percent of students said they work on weekends.

Unit 3 Dream vacation

Language focus Pages 34 and 35

1. Vacation destinations

B Track 11

1. **Woman:** Borneo is a fantastic vacation destination. It's an island located in Southeast Asia, and as anyone who's been there knows, it's one of the most exotic locations in the world. Visitors to Borneo can enjoy lots of interesting attractions. It's known for its rare wildlife, thick jungles, and tropical rain forests. Borneo is a great place to discover nature firsthand.

2. **Man:** Maui is a great place for a relaxing beach vacation. It's a Hawaiian island that's situated northwest of the Big Island, and it's one of the world's most beautiful places. Maui is known for its peaceful white sand beaches and amazing natural scenery. It offers fabulous accommodations including several luxurious five-star resorts. So, what are you waiting for? Let's go to Maui!

3. **Woman:** Rome, the capital city of Italy, is a vacation destination no one should miss. Rome is located right in the middle of Italy, and it's one of the most romantic cities on Earth. It's known for ancient ruins and fantastic museums, and it also offers excellent restaurants. Choose Rome as your vacation destination and you won't be disappointed.

2. Activities and accommodations

A Track 12

1. **Woman:** You'll have an opportunity to hike through the jungle on a two-day tour. You'll travel upriver by boat where you'll be able to watch endangered orangutans in their natural habitat. And you'll have a chance to go on a night safari and hear the sounds of the rain forest wildlife. You'll stay at a rain forest campsite in simple

tents made completely of natural, local materials. It's a true eco-experience.

2. **Man:** You can relax and get a tan at the hotel's private beach. You'll have a chance to spend time shopping at some of the island's most popular boutiques. And if you're in the mood for an adventure, you'll have an opportunity to watch the sunset from the top of Haleakala volcano. You'll stay at the Maui Oceanfront Resort, a luxurious five-star resort. Doesn't that sound like paradise?

3. **Woman:** You'll have a chance to learn about world-famous Italian art and architecture. You can take a sightseeing tour around the city by bus. You'll also be able to visit the countryside on a trip to the lovely Tivoli Gardens, located about forty minutes from the center of Rome. We'll spend one night in a charming bed-and-breakfast with fabulous views of the gardens. This vacation is a fascinating historical journey.

Organization focus Page 37

2. Sam's outline

Presentation focus Page 38

4. Sam's presentation

Track 13

Sam: Are you looking for some excitement? Do you want to experience exotic cultures? If your answer is yes, then I have the perfect vacation for you. It's the South Island Adventure, an outdoor nature trek. This is perfect for people who want an exciting, active vacation.

The South Island of New Zealand is located near Australia in the beautiful Pacific Ocean. It's one of the most fascinating places in the world. The South Island is known for its national parks, picturesque countryside, and exotic plants and wildlife. It also offers stunning mountain views and clear blue ocean water.

On this trip, you can hike through Kahurangi National Park, which is situated in the northwest part of the South Island. You'll be able to explore deep caves and rich forests. You can learn about the amazing wildlife, including birds and insects that are found nowhere else in the world. You'll have a chance to see New Zealand's national symbol, the kiwi bird, too! You'll also have an opportunity to experience ancient Maori culture while paddling on a river in a traditional Maori canoe, and you can visit a traditional Maori meetinghouse. On your last day, you'll be able to go whale watching and swim with dolphins.

The accommodations on this trip will be unforgettable. On the first and last nights, you'll stay in a luxurious four-star hotel in Christchurch. Then, during the trek, you'll spend six nights in a cozy bed-and-breakfast near the park, with all meals included. New Zealand is known for its friendly people, and the family you'll stay with will make you feel very welcome.

Does this sound like a dream vacation? I think it does! The cost is $1,200 for eight nights. This vacation includes seven days of educational outdoor activities and breathtaking natural scenery. It's a wonderful opportunity to explore the great outdoors. So, what are you waiting for? It's time to go on a South Island Adventure!

Unit 4 How the world works

Language focus Pages 46 and 47

1. Introducing a process presentation

A, B Track 14

1. **Kazu:** On average, most people sleep for about eight hours a night. That means we spend about one-third of our lives sleeping! However, most people have no idea what happens during the sleep cycle. In this talk, I'll go over what the stages of sleep are called and when dreams are created in the sleep cycle. I'll also discuss how the brain is affected by sleep – and by lack of sleep.

2. **Tami:** The largest wave ever recorded hit the coast of Alaska in 1958. The water reached areas 530 meters above sea level. That's higher than some of the world's tallest buildings! Tsunamis are huge, powerful waves that can cause incredible destruction, and tsunami formation is a fascinating process. In this presentation, I'll go over which places are most often affected by tsunamis and discuss what kinds of damage are caused when a tsunami hits. I'll also explain the process of how the waves are formed.

2. How does it happen?

A Track 15

1. **Kazu:** All right. Now I'll go over the sleep cycle and what really happens when we sleep. The first stage is the drowsiness stage. This is when the eyes first close, and you begin to feel sleepy. The second stage is the light sleep stage. During this stage, the heart rate is lowered. Then, the next stage is the deep sleep stage. At this point, the brain waves are slowed. The final stage in the cycle is the REM sleep stage. This is when dreaming begins.

2. **Tami:** Now I'll explain how tsunamis are formed. In the first stage, there is an underwater earthquake. This is when the ocean floor moves suddenly. In the second stage, layers of earth are pushed together. At this point, the water level rises slightly above normal. In the next stage, waves are created and start to move toward shore. During this stage, the waves gain speed and strength. In the final stage, the waves hit shore. This is when houses and buildings are often destroyed.

Organization focus Page 49

2. Nicole's outline

Presentation focus Page 50

4. Nicole's presentation

Track 16

Nicole: These days we're never far from a coffee shop. There's one on almost every street corner. Did you know that coffee is the second-most traded product in the world,

after oil? In this talk, I'll explain how coffee beans are grown and harvested, and I'll go over how the raw beans are processed and turned into the delicious drink many of us enjoy every morning. I'll be happy to take your questions when I'm finished. OK, let's get started.

The first stage of coffee manufacturing is the growing and harvesting stage. During this stage, the coffee trees produce small red berries called coffee cherries. About five years after a new tree is planted, the coffee cherries are ready to be harvested. At this point, the coffee cherries are picked either by hand or machine.

The second stage is the processing stage. This is when the red coffee cherries are changed into green coffee beans. During this stage, the outer fruit is removed from the coffee cherries, so only the coffee seeds, or beans, are left. The beans are then dried, sorted, and put into cloth sacks for shipping.

The next stage, or third stage, is the roasting stage. During this stage, the beans are placed in a roasting machine and heated to around 240 degrees Celsius. The length of roasting time determines the beans' color and richness.

The final stage of coffee manufacturing is the grinding and brewing stage. This is when the whole beans are crushed into a powder and mixed with hot water to make a cup of coffee. There are different methods of grinding and brewing, depending on how strong you want the coffee to taste.

That completes the coffee-manufacturing process: growing and harvesting the coffee cherries, processing the fruit, roasting the beans, and finally, grinding and brewing the coffee. For those of you who'd like to find out more, I recommend reading *Coffee: A Cultural History from Around the World* by Ed Milton. Thank you. We have a few minutes left. I'll be glad to take your questions now.

Unit 5 In my opinion

Language focus Pages 58 and 59

1. Expressing opinions

B, C Track 17

1. **Alex:** Did you wear a uniform when you went to school? Many students these days don't like school uniforms. They say that uniforms are bad because they make everyone look the same, and students lose their individual identities. However, in my opinion, uniforms should be required for all students. This is because wearing school uniforms saves students money, and it improves students' schoolwork.

2. **Elena:** Chances are you have a computer and you use the Internet. More and more people are using the Internet today, including young children. Most people believe that the Internet can be a useful learning tool for kids. But I don't think that young kids should use it unless a parent is with them. I feel this way because the Internet is still not controlled enough to protect children, and many kids don't know the risks, so it can be dangerous.

3. **Lisa:** As university students, we all have busy schedules. Studying, playing sports, working part-time jobs . . . There isn't much free time in our days. However, I feel strongly that university students should do volunteer work. Even just a few hours a month can be a great experience. Volunteer work is very educational, and students can learn a lot from getting involved in the community. In addition, helping other people is extremely rewarding.

2. Supporting opinions

A Track 18

1. **Alex:** It's a fact that young people these days spend a lot of money on clothes. Did you know that some teens spend up to one hundred dollars a month on clothes? I'm a teacher, and in my experience, when students pay too much attention to fashion, it definitely affects their schoolwork in a negative way. Wearing uniforms also means that differences between social groups are less obvious, which is a very good thing in the classroom.

2. **Elena:** Did you know that many kids think it's OK to share personal information online? According to researchers, 75 percent of children say it's OK to share information online about themselves and their family in exchange for goods or services. That's a large percentage, but in my experience, supervising kids' Internet use can help parents worry a lot less. Using the Internet with your kids is also a great way to spend time doing something together.

3. **Lisa:** An article I read last year said that only 10 percent of people volunteer. In my experience, volunteering is a valuable opportunity to get work experience, and it can help people find jobs. Here's an example that supports my opinion: A friend of mine graduated last year. He had never worked, and even though he was a good student, he had trouble finding a job. He told me he wished he had volunteered and gotten some experience when he was in school.

Organization focus Page 61
2. Chris's outline

Presentation focus Page 62
4. Chris's presentation

Track 19

Chris: We all enjoy a good meal, and I know that for many of you, that includes eating meat. Hamburgers are tasty, and there's nothing like a good steak or some fried chicken. However, I believe that people should stop eating meat. Yes. In my opinion, everyone should become a vegetarian! There are three good reasons to support this view. It's good for your health, and it saves money. Also, eating a vegetarian diet helps the environment.

First, let's consider health. It's a fact that a vegetarian diet is healthier than one that includes meat. According to health experts, people who eat meat have higher rates of heart disease. In my experience, eating a vegetarian diet can make a big difference. I stopped eating meat a year

ago, and I lost about five kilos in the first two months. I now have a lot more energy and I feel great about myself.

Now let's think about money. Did you know that meat is the most expensive part of your diet? That's right. Meat products cost around three times as much as an equal amount of vegetables. Just imagine how much money you'd save by cutting meat from your shopping list.

Another reason to support a vegetarian diet is to help the environment, such as the rain forest. An article I read said that some meat industries cut down large sections of the rain forest in Central and South America in order to create more land to raise animals for meat. In fact, about 25 percent of the rain forest in Central America has been destroyed since 1960. Our planet needs the rain forests, and cutting them down will hurt everyone.

In conclusion, I believe that a vegetarian diet is the best choice. You'll be healthier, you'll save a lot of money, and you'll be helping the environment. Of course, I know it's not easy to give up something you enjoy. It wasn't easy for me at first. But I made the right choice, and I hope you will, too – for yourself and for the world! Thank you.

Presentation skills focus Pages 64 and 65
1. Emphasizing an opposing opinion

A Track 20

1. **Alex:** Many students don't like school uniforms. However, in my opinion, uniforms should be required for all students.

2. **Elena:** Most people believe that the Internet can be a useful learning tool for kids. But I don't think that young kids should use the Internet unless a parent is with them.

3. **Lisa:** As university students, we all have busy schedules. However, I feel strongly that university students should do volunteer work.

B Track 21

1. **Man:** Many people say that recycling should be a personal choice. However, I believe that recycling should be required by law.

2. **Woman:** We all understand that paying taxes is the duty of all citizens. But in my opinion, only very wealthy people should pay taxes.

3. **Woman:** We all know that TV advertising aimed at children is very effective. But I feel strongly that advertising aimed at children should be banned.

4. **Man:** Most people think that school is the best place for young people to get an education. However, in my opinion, traveling is more educational than going to school.

2. Your turn

A Track 22

Man: None of us likes the idea of giving up our cars. However, I feel strongly that people should stop driving cars. According to experts, we're using more oil than ever before, and pollution from cars hurts the environment. Many people believe that ethanol will power our cars in the future. But I don't believe that ethanol is the solution. In my opinion, we need to make lifestyle changes. I think that people should use public transportation more, and many of us can walk or ride a bike to work or school. In my experience, it isn't too hard to give up driving.

Unit 6 In the news

Language focus Pages 70 and 71
1. Introducing news stories
B Track 23

1. **Mei:** Do you know how long it took for the world population to go from one billion to two billion? Was it ten years? 50 years? 100? Last week, I read a fascinating article in the magazine *World Matters* and it looked at recent population trends in different countries. Today, I'll outline the main points of the article and then I'll give you my reaction. At the end I'll ask for your comments and opinions.

2. **Jeff:** I'm sure that everyone in the world wants to be happy. But how many of us are truly happy? I saw a thought-provoking report on TV last night that looked at our stressful modern lifestyles and the effects this stress has on people's levels of happiness. It also talked about what makes people happy – not just for a short time, but for the long term, too. First, I'm going to summarize the main points, and then I'll tell you how I feel about it. At the end I'll ask for your comments and opinions.

3. **Luis:** I guess a lot of us enjoy a fast-food meal sometimes, right? Well, I read an astonishing article on the Internet a few days ago. It talked about the new fast-food warnings, and it explained that some officials think that the government should have the power to control people's eating habits. Today, I'm going to outline the main points of the article, and then I'll tell you how I feel about it. At the end you'll have a chance to share your opinion.

2. The details
A, B Track 24

1. **Mei:** According to the article, the world population reached one billion in 1800, and it took more than 100 years to get to two billion. But it took just thirteen years for the world's population to go from five to six billion! Currently, Latin America has the fastest population growth, which means there may soon be too many people there. But the article reported that some places have the opposite problem. Some countries in Asia, for example, Japan and South Korea, have very low birthrates, so their populations are beginning to decline.

2. **Jeff:** According to the report, most people feel that money is somewhat important for happiness, but only until they have the basic things all humans need, for example, food and shelter. After that, the report said that having more money doesn't usually make people any happier. It said that the keys to happiness were being active, being effective, and having good relationships. It went on to say that in today's society, men tend to be happier than women. This is because many women say they often feel overwhelmed by the demands of both work and family.

3. **Luis:** How can the government control our eating habits? Well, the article stated that most officials don't support a fast-food tax, but it went on to say that the government may put warnings on unhealthy foods, for example, foods with a lot of sugar, salt, or fat. According to the article, the warnings would encourage people to think about what they eat and to choose healthier foods. There are a lot of people with health problems caused by bad diets, who cost our health system a lot of money.

Organization focus Page 73
2. Mari's outline

Presentation focus Page 74
4. Mari's presentation
Track 25

Mari: Think for a second. Can you imagine living on two U.S. dollars a day? Well, you may be surprised to hear this. Half the world's population – three billion people – lives on less than two dollars a day! The other day, I read a disturbing story in a newsmagazine. It talked about poverty in the world and what can be done about it. Today, I'll outline the main points of the story, and then I'll tell you how I feel about it. At the end you'll have a chance to share your opinion.

So, what did I find out? According to the article, the three richest people in the world have more wealth than the 48 poorest countries in the world. That's one quarter of all the world's countries! The article also said that one in two children lives in poverty – a shocking statistic. And it went on to say that 27,000 children die every day from extreme poverty – that's one child every three seconds!

The article also looked at education. It said that one billion people entered the 21st century unable to read or sign their names. The article stated that 10 billion dollars would be enough to put every child into school. That's a lot of money, but did you know that it's less than one percent of what the world spends every year on arms?

Well, I'm glad to say that the news in the article wasn't all bad. It went on to say that there are many nongovernmental organizations and charities that are helping poor people, and that some businesses and corporations are also helping. For example, have you heard of Product Red? Did you know that if you buy a Product Red iPod, Apple gives a portion of the purchase price to the Global Fund, which helps fight disease in Africa? And it doesn't cost you anything extra!

I think this story is shocking and moving. It made me feel hopeful, however, when I read about the work of the charity organizations. Maybe I can't do a lot myself, but if we all help a little, it'll make a big difference. Now I'd like to hear your views on this topic, especially your ideas about what we can do to help people who are living in poverty.

Presentation skills focus Page 76

1. Leading a group discussion

Track 26

Open

Woman: Now I'd like to hear your views.
I'd like to invite you to share your ideas.
Now it's your turn to voice your opinions.

Continue

Woman: Can anyone add to that?
Do you all agree?
What do you think, Mark?

Close

Woman: We've heard a lot of great ideas today.
That's all the time we have. Thanks for sharing your views.
Thank you for participating today.